1 WORLD MANGA

PASSAGE
3

1 WORLD MANGA #3

Story by Annette Roman
Art by Leandro Ng
Ink by Walden Wong

Tone/Leandro Ng
Lettering & Sound Effects/Sabrina Heep
Cover & Interior Design/Courtney Utt
Logo Design/Mark Wasserman
Back Matter/Patricia Katayama

1 World Manga is a joint project of VIZ Media, LLC and The World Bank.

Managing Editor/Annette Roman
Director of Production/Noboru Watanabe
VP of Publishing/Alvin Lu
VP of Sales & Marketing/Liza Coppola
Publisher/Hyoe Narita

Printed in Canada

Published by VIZ Media, LLC/The World Bank

VIZ Media, LLC
P.O. Box 77010
San Francisco, CA 94107

The International Bank for Reconstruction and Development/The World Bank
1818 H Street NW
Washington DC 20433
Telephone: 202-473-1000
Internet: www.worldbank.org
E-mail: feedback@worldbank.org

10 9 8 7 6 5 4 3 2 1
First printing, March 2006

  THE WORLD BANK

www.viz.com
store.viz.com

PASSAGE 3

GLOBAL WARMING–
THE LAGOON OF THE
VANISHING FISH

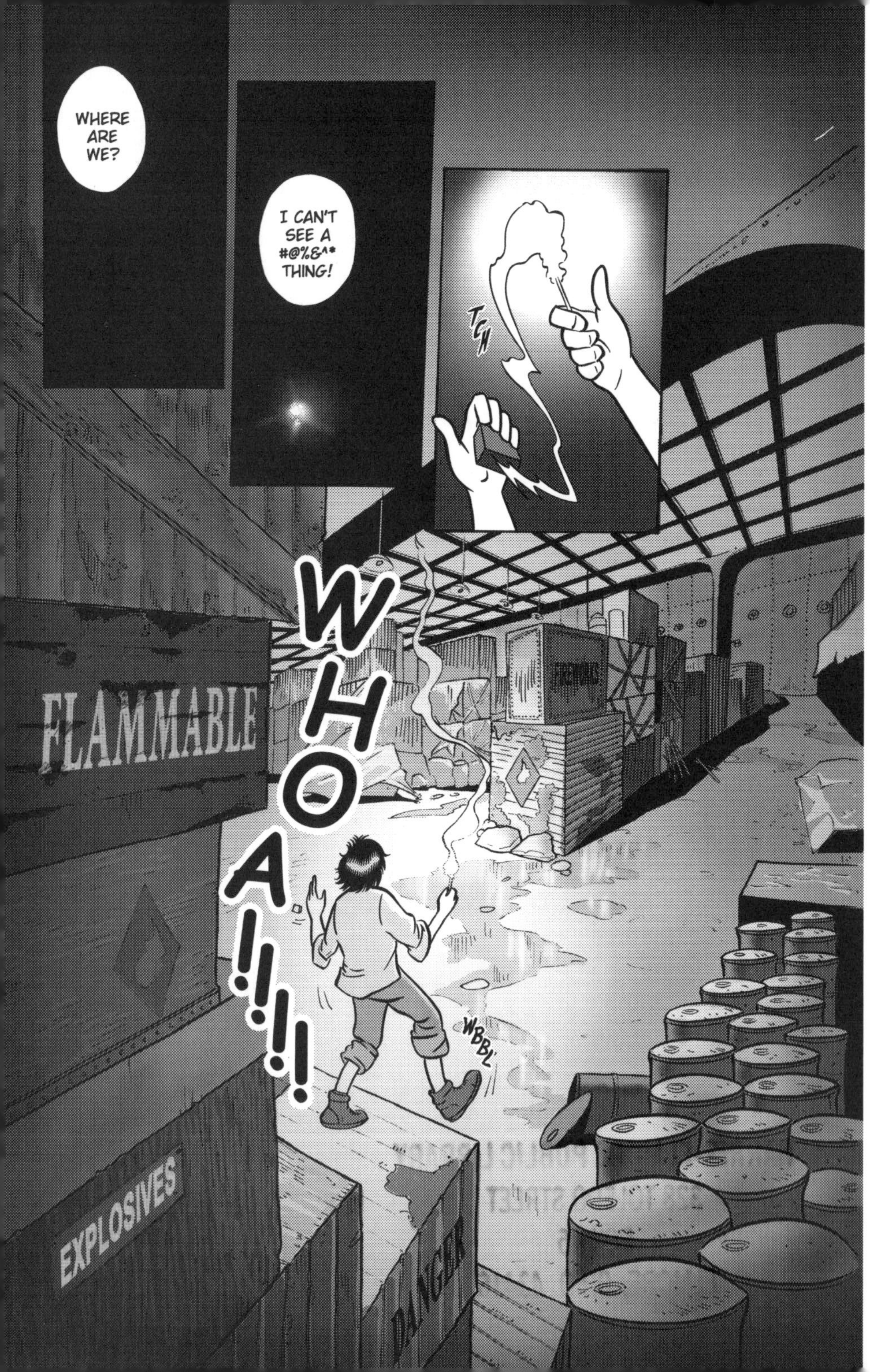
WHERE ARE WE?
I CAN'T SEE A #@%&^* THING!
TCH
FLAMMABLE
WHOA!!!!!
WBBL
EXPLOSIVES
DANGER

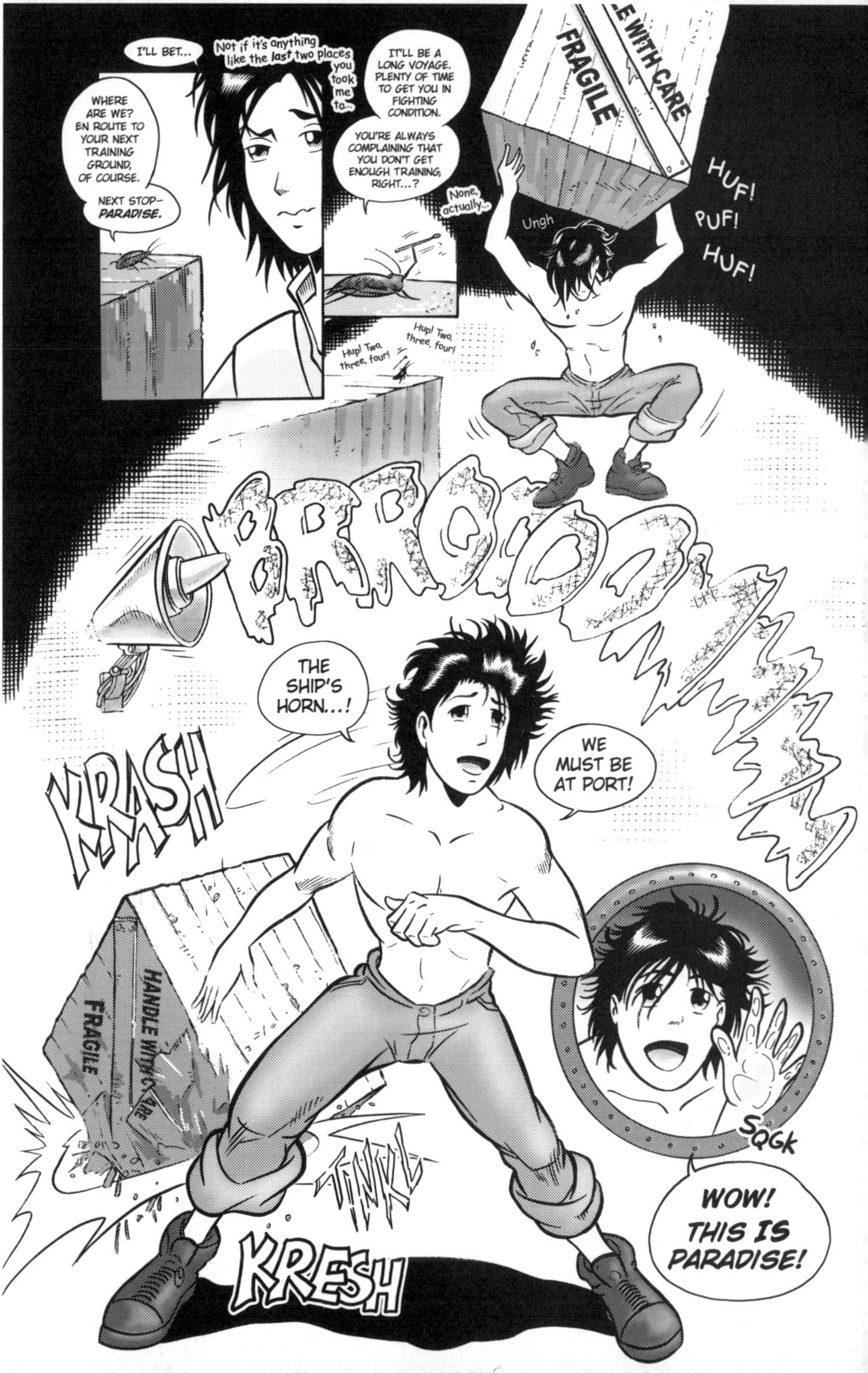
WHERE ARE WE?
EN ROUTE TO YOUR NEXT TRAINING GROUND, OF COURSE.
NEXT STOP— PARADISE.
I'LL BET...
Not if it's anything like the last two places you took me to...
IT'LL BE A LONG VOYAGE. PLENTY OF TIME TO GET YOU IN FIGHTING CONDITION.
YOU'RE ALWAYS COMPLAINING THAT YOU DON'T GET ENOUGH TRAINING, RIGHT...?
None, actually...
LE WITH CARE
FRAGILE
Ungh
HUF! PUF! HUF!
Hup! Two, three, four!
Hup! Two, three, four!
THE SHIP'S HORN...!
WE MUST BE AT PORT!
KRASH
HANDLE WITH C RE
FRAGILE
TINKL
KRESH
SQGk
WOW! THIS IS PARADISE!

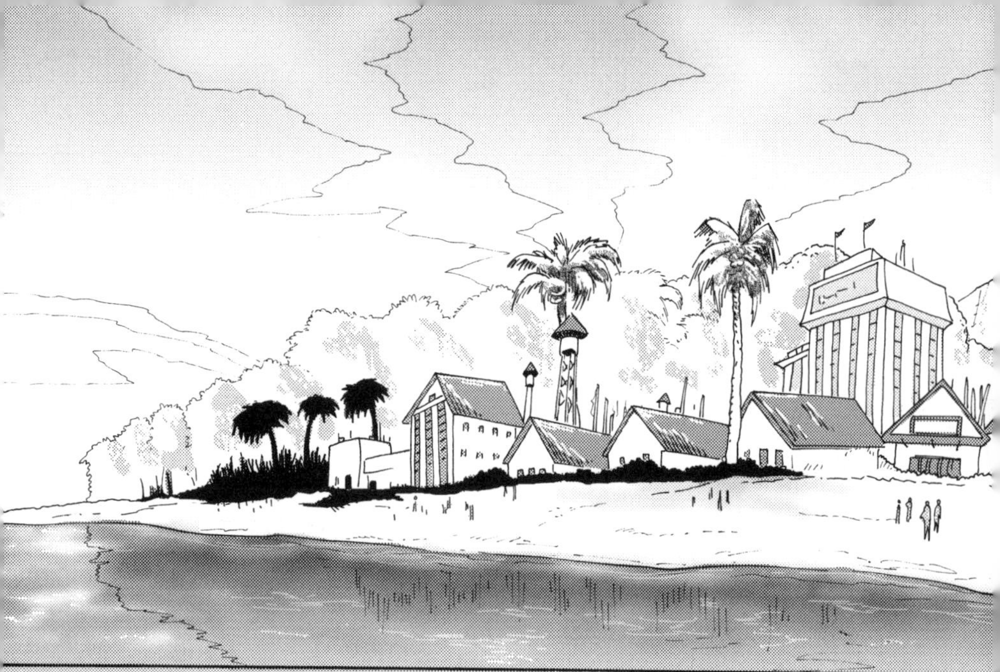

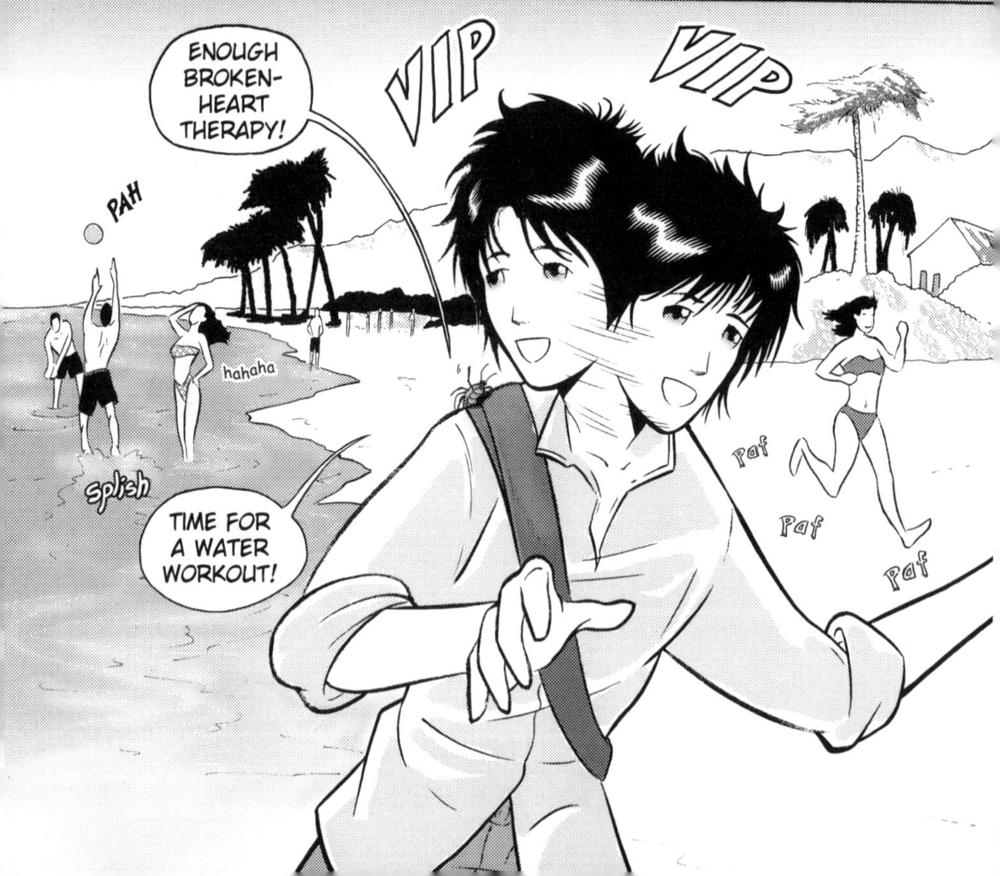
ENOUGH BROKEN-HEART THERAPY!
VIP
VIP
PAH
hahaha
splish
TIME FOR A WATER WORKOUT!
paf
paf
paf

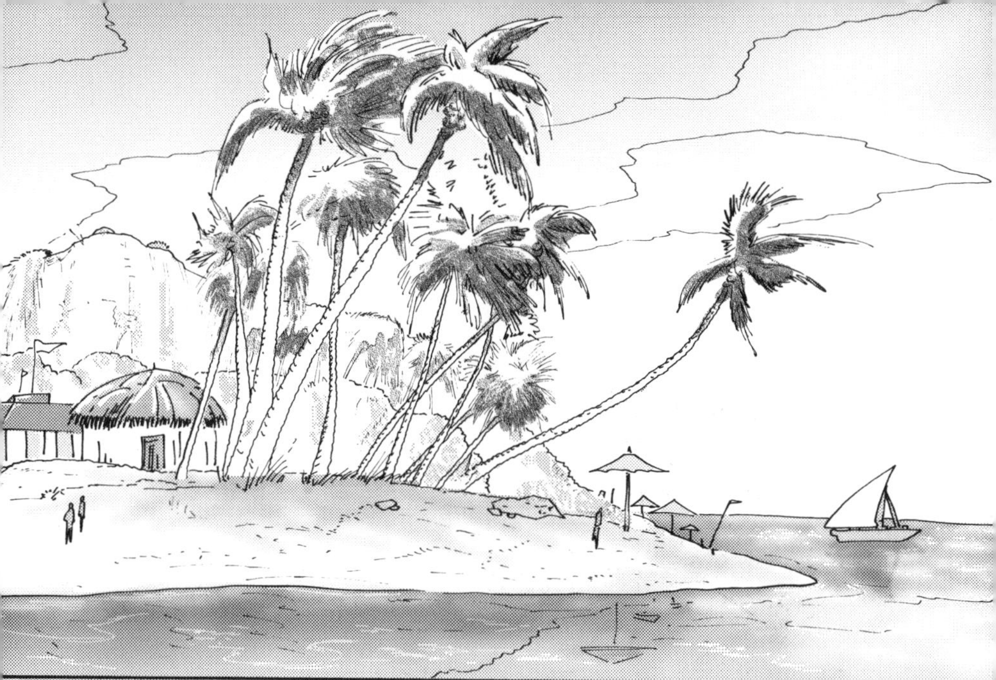

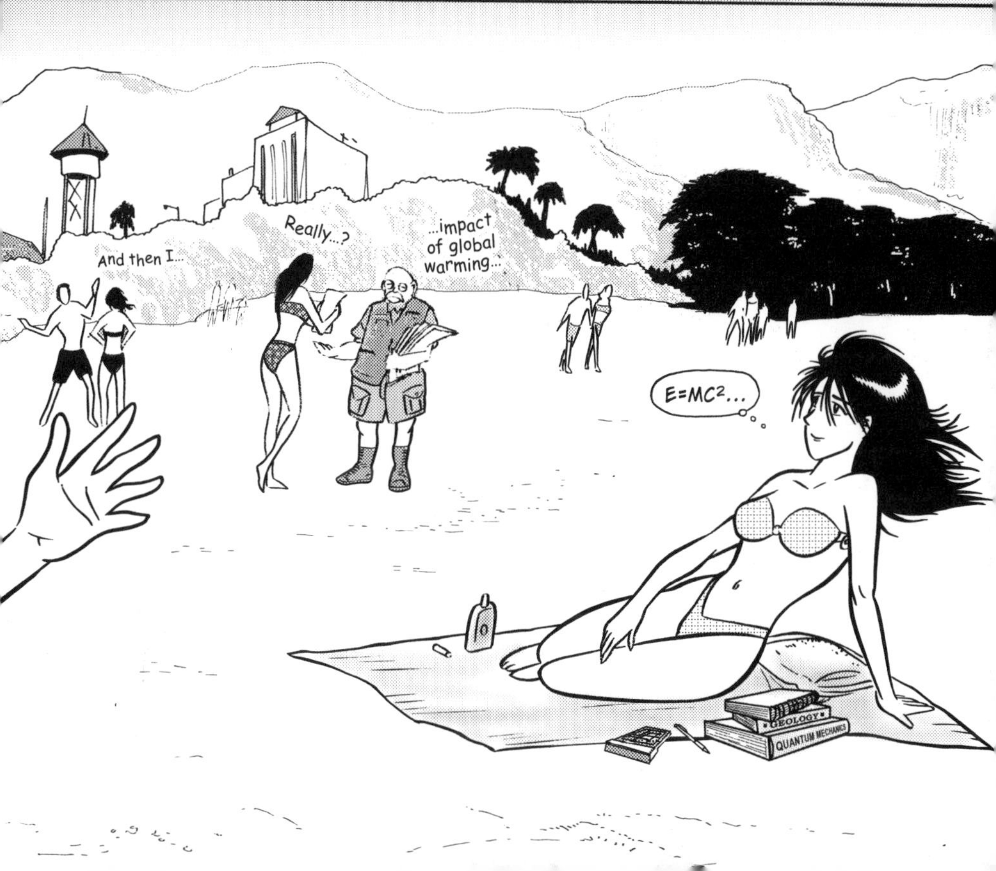

And then I...
Really...?
...impact of global warming...
E=MC²...
GEOLOGY
QUANTUM MECHANICS

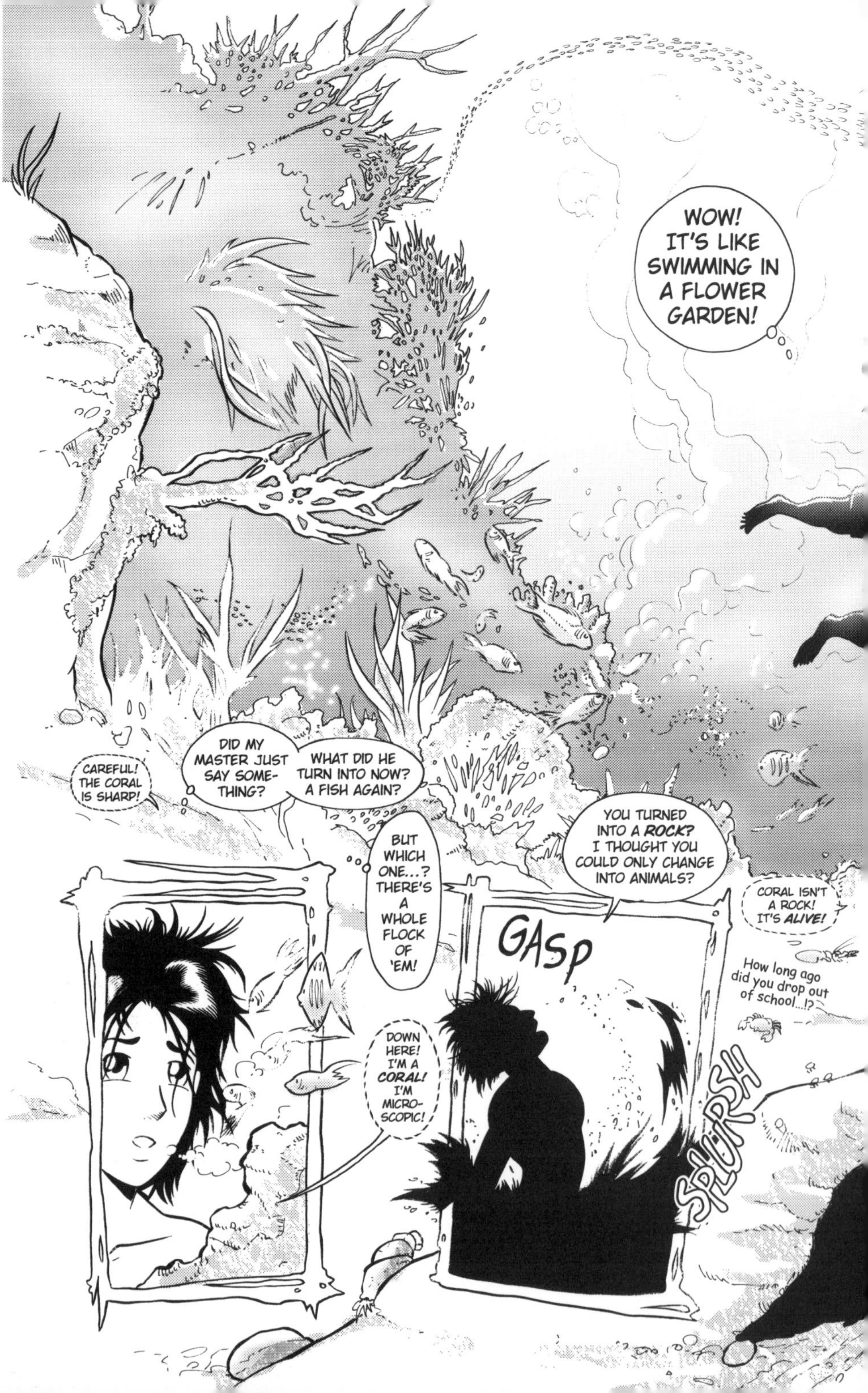
WOW! IT'S LIKE SWIMMING IN A FLOWER GARDEN!
CAREFUL! THE CORAL IS SHARP!
DID MY MASTER JUST SAY SOME-THING?
WHAT DID HE TURN INTO NOW? A FISH AGAIN?
BUT WHICH ONE...? THERE'S A WHOLE FLOCK OF 'EM!
DOWN HERE! I'M A CORAL! I'M MICRO-SCOPIC!
YOU TURNED INTO A ROCK? I THOUGHT YOU COULD ONLY CHANGE INTO ANIMALS?
GASP
CORAL ISN'T A ROCK! IT'S ALIVE!
How long ago did you drop out of school...!?
SPLURSH

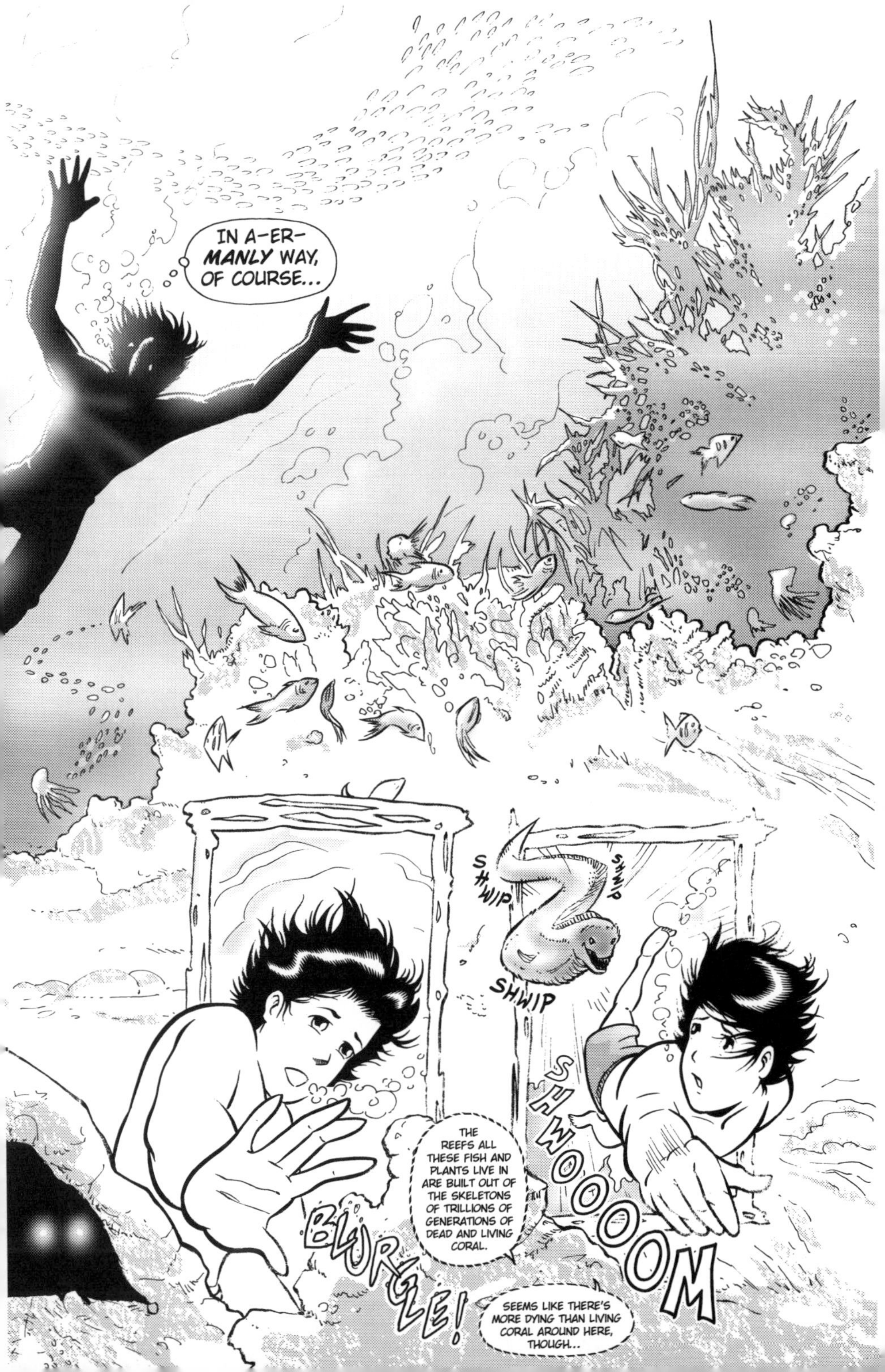
IN A-ER- MANLY WAY, OF COURSE...
SHWIP
SHWIP
SHWIP
THE REEFS ALL THESE FISH AND PLANTS LIVE IN ARE BUILT OUT OF THE SKELETONS OF TRILLIONS OF GENERATIONS OF DEAD AND LIVING CORAL.
SHWOOOOM
BLURGLE!
SEEMS LIKE THERE'S MORE DYING THAN LIVING CORAL AROUND HERE, THOUGH...

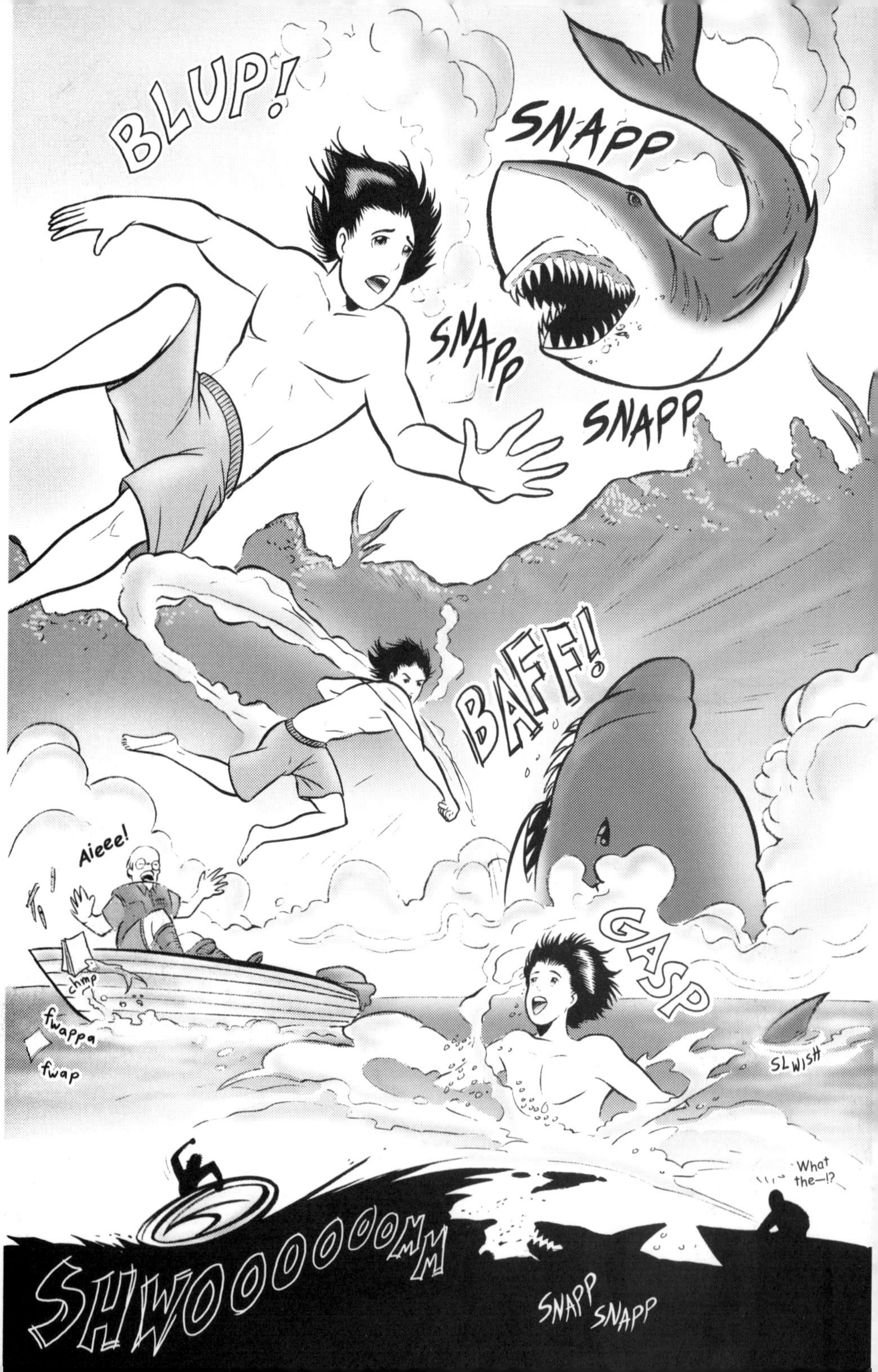
BLUP!
SNAPP
SNAPP
SNAPP
BAFF!
Aieee!
chmp
fwappa
fwap
GASP
SLWISH
What the—!?
SHWOOOOOOOMMM
SNAPP
SNAPP

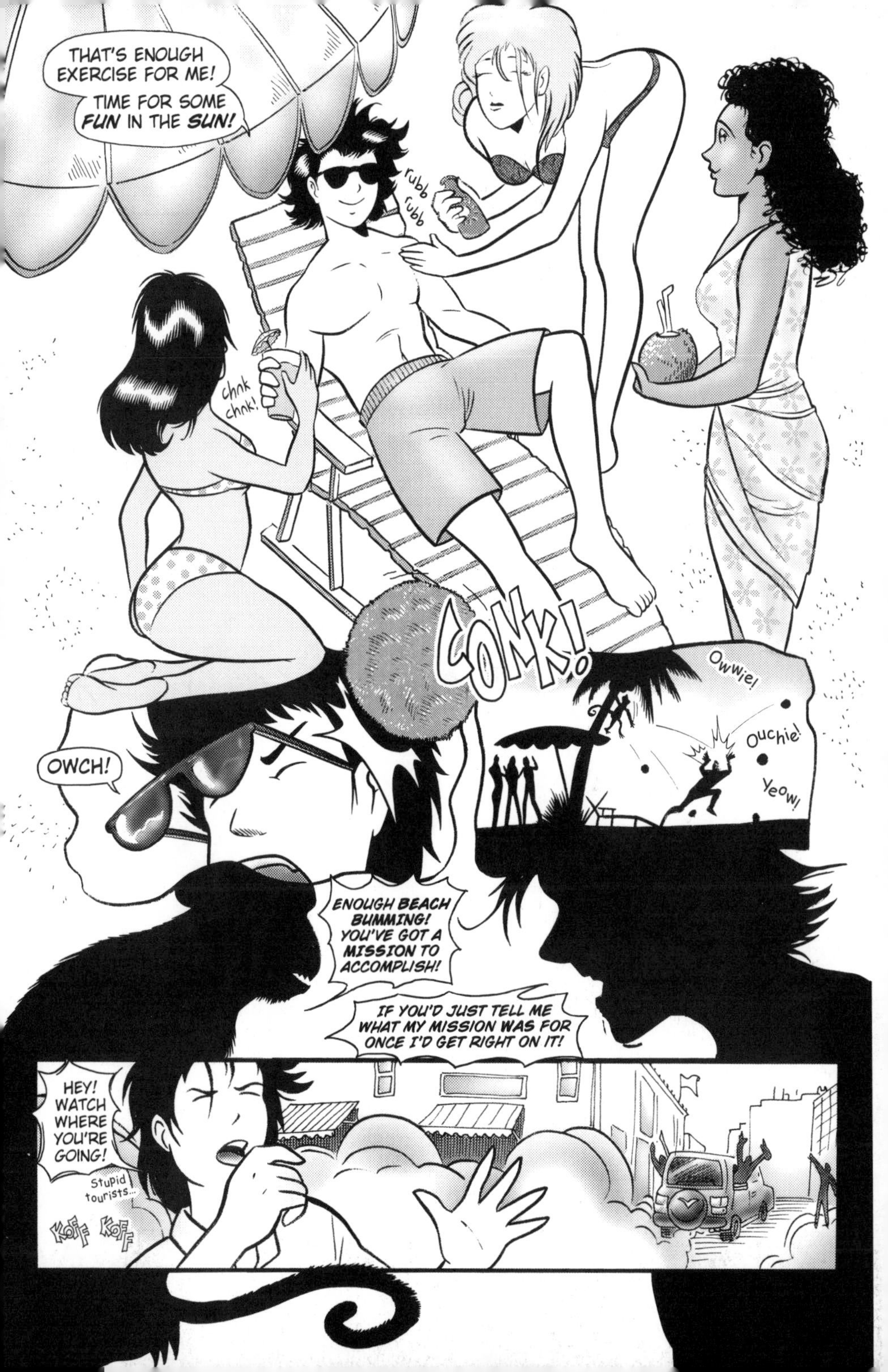
THAT'S ENOUGH EXERCISE FOR ME!
TIME FOR SOME FUN IN THE SUN!
rubb rubb
chnk chnk!
CONK!
OWCH!
Owwie!
Ouchie!
Yeow!
ENOUGH BEACH BUMMING! YOU'VE GOT A MISSION TO ACCOMPLISH!
IF YOU'D JUST TELL ME WHAT MY MISSION WAS FOR ONCE I'D GET RIGHT ON IT!
HEY! WATCH WHERE YOU'RE GOING!
Stupid tourists...
KOFF KOFF

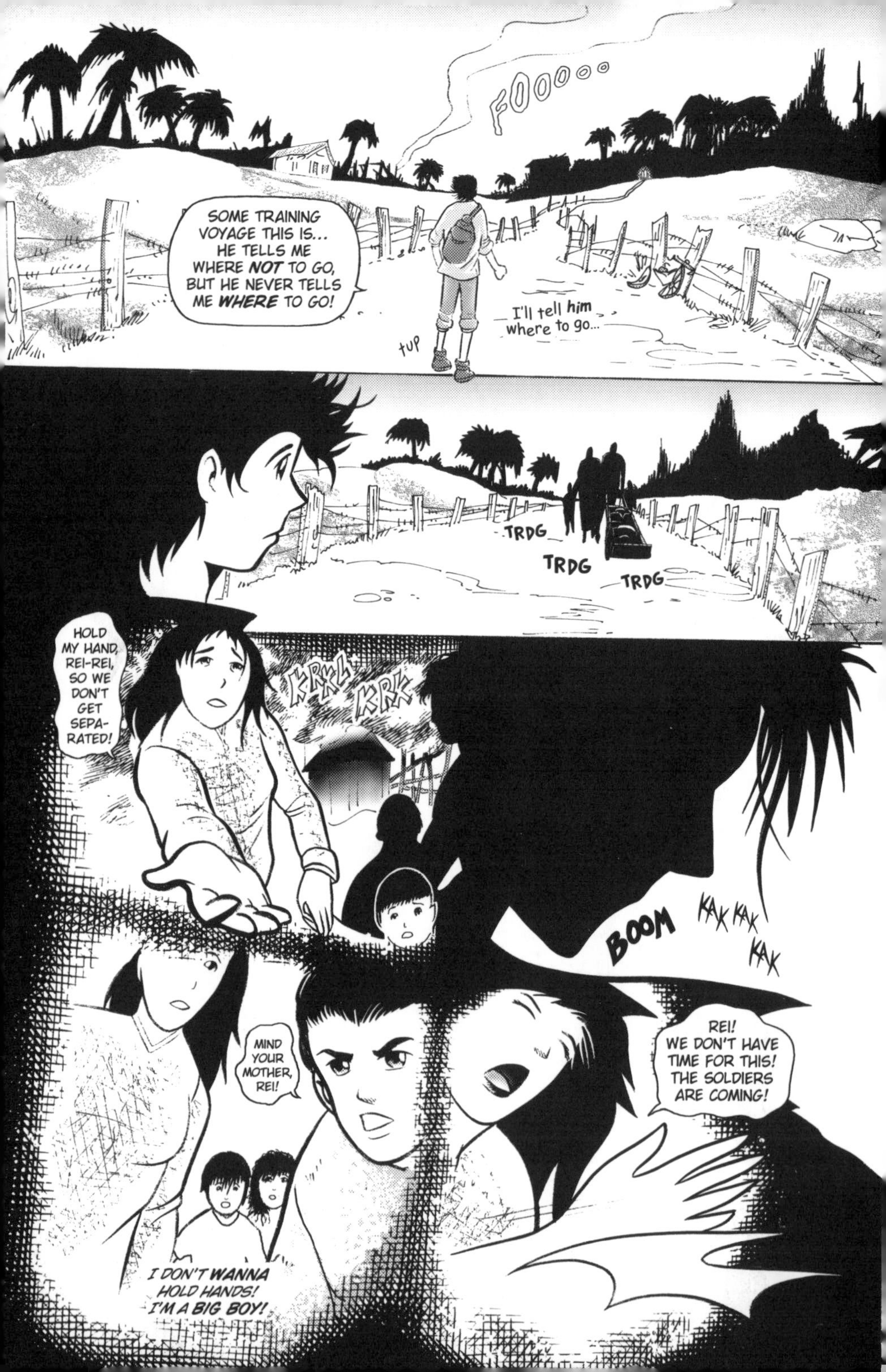
FOOOOO
SOME TRAINING VOYAGE THIS IS... HE TELLS ME WHERE NOT TO GO, BUT HE NEVER TELLS ME WHERE TO GO!
I'll tell him where to go...
TUP
TRDG
TRDG
TRDG
HOLD MY HAND, REI-REI, SO WE DON'T GET SEPA-RATED!
KRKL KRK
BOOM
KAK KAK KAK
REI! WE DON'T HAVE TIME FOR THIS! THE SOLDIERS ARE COMING!
MIND YOUR MOTHER, REI!
I DON'T WANNA HOLD HANDS! I'M A BIG BOY!

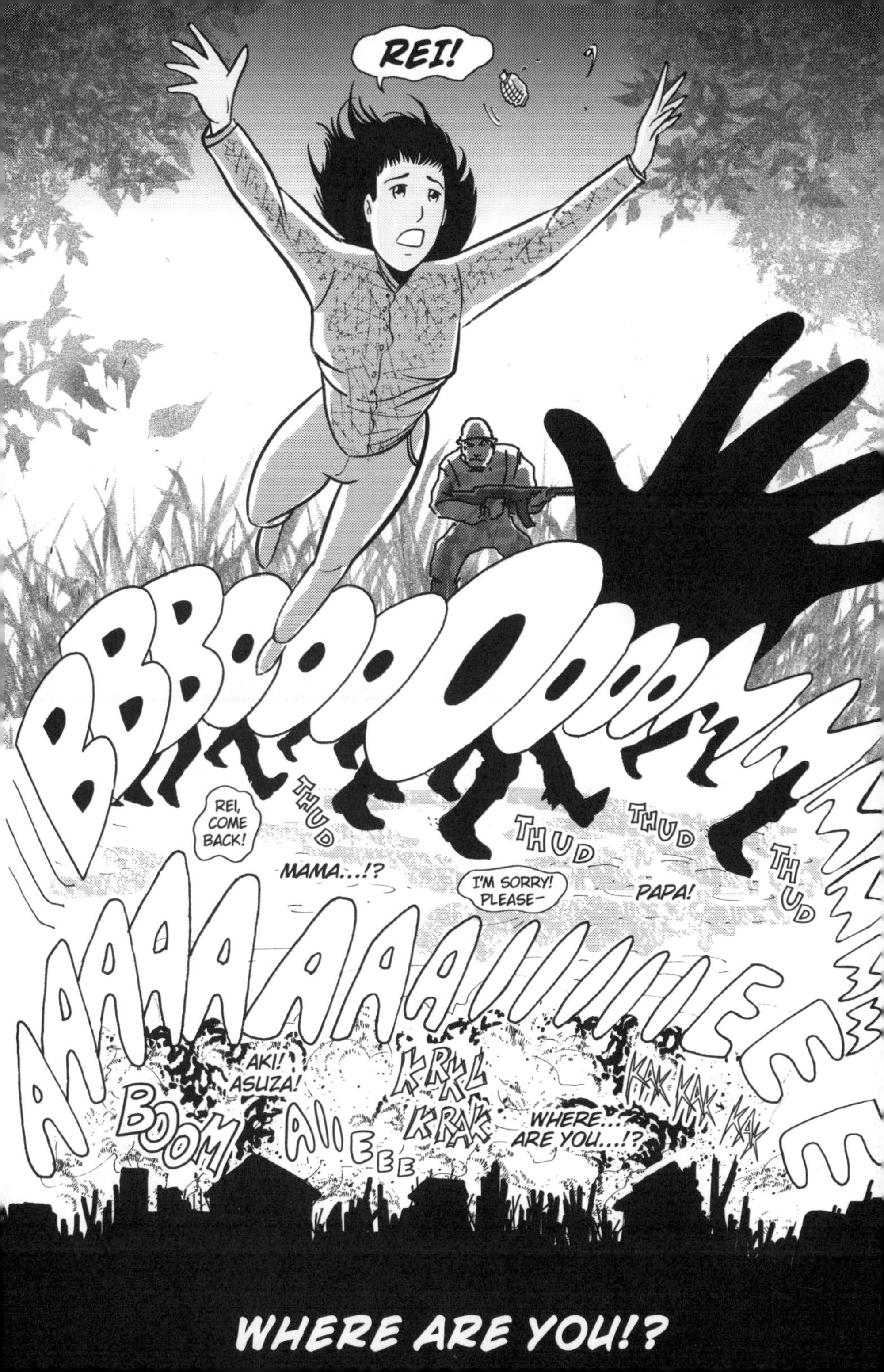

REI!
BBBOOOOOOOOOMM
REI, COME BACK!
THUD
MAMA...!?
THUD
I'M SORRY! PLEASE–
THUD
PAPA!
THUD
AAAAAAAAIIIIIIEEEE
AKI! ASUZA!
BOOOM
AIIEEE
KRKL
KRAK
WHERE... ARE YOU...!?
KAK KAK KAK
WHERE ARE YOU!?

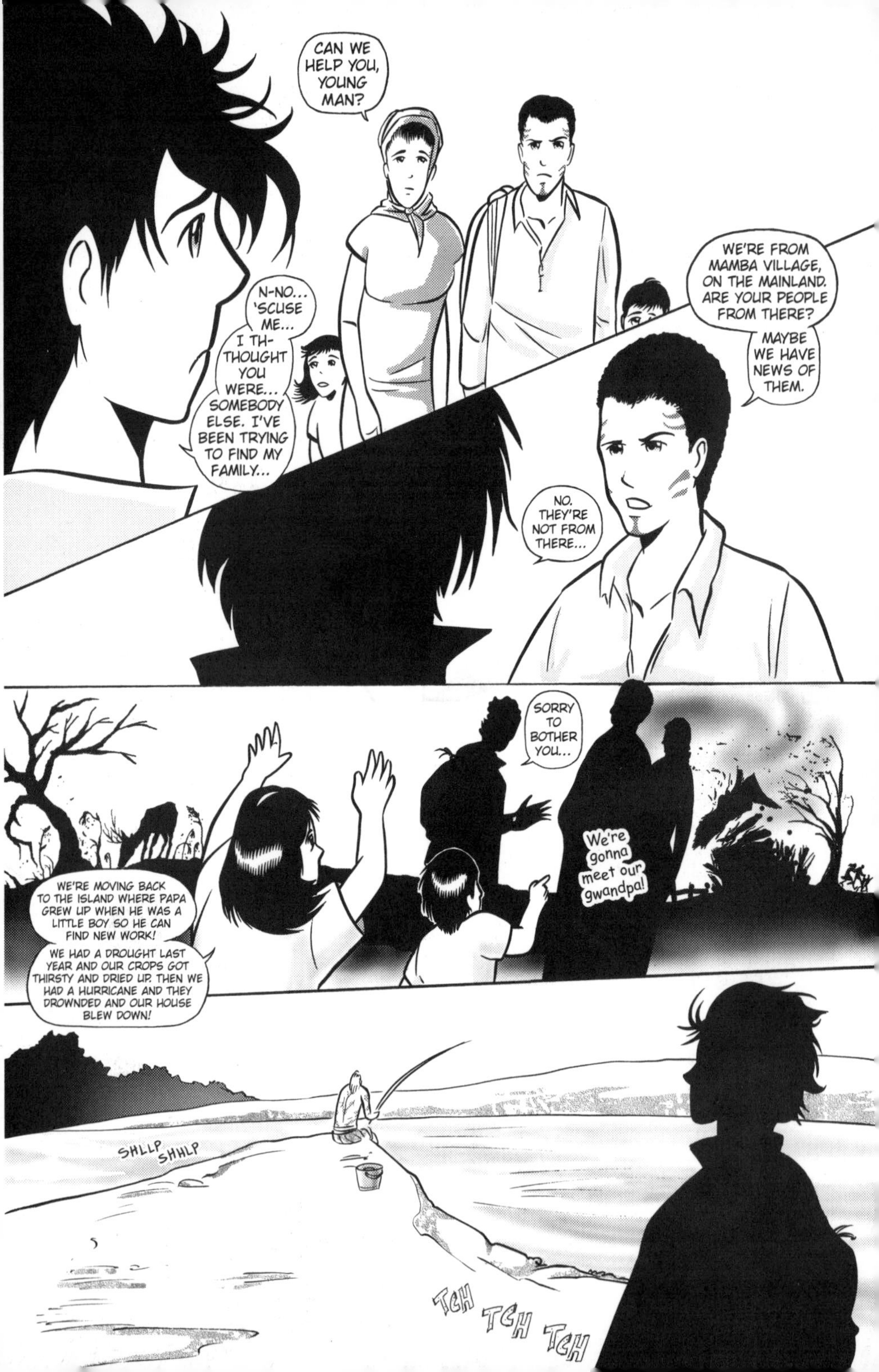
CAN WE HELP YOU, YOUNG MAN?
N-NO... 'SCUSE ME... I TH-THOUGHT YOU WERE... SOMEBODY ELSE. I'VE BEEN TRYING TO FIND MY FAMILY...
WE'RE FROM MAMBA VILLAGE, ON THE MAINLAND. ARE YOUR PEOPLE FROM THERE?
MAYBE WE HAVE NEWS OF THEM.
NO. THEY'RE NOT FROM THERE...
SORRY TO BOTHER YOU...
We're gonna meet our gwandpa!
WE'RE MOVING BACK TO THE ISLAND WHERE PAPA GREW UP WHEN HE WAS A LITTLE BOY SO HE CAN FIND NEW WORK!
WE HAD A DROUGHT LAST YEAR AND OUR CROPS GOT THIRSTY AND DRIED UP. THEN WE HAD A HURRICANE AND THEY DROWNED AND OUR HOUSE BLEW DOWN!
SHLLP SHHLP
TCH TCH TCH

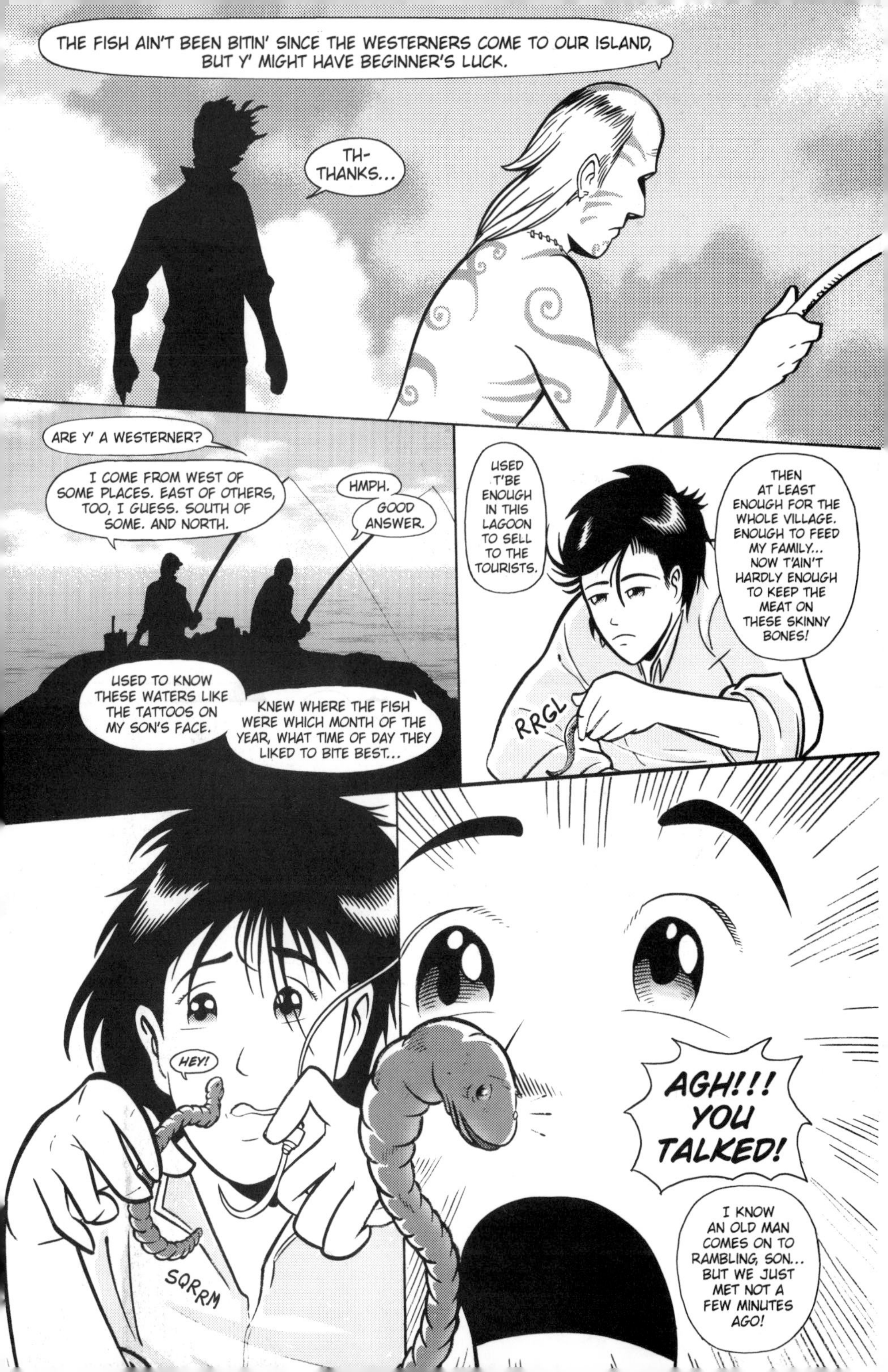
THE FISH AIN'T BEEN BITIN' SINCE THE WESTERNERS COME TO OUR ISLAND, BUT Y' MIGHT HAVE BEGINNER'S LUCK.
TH- THANKS...
ARE Y' A WESTERNER?
I COME FROM WEST OF SOME PLACES. EAST OF OTHERS, TOO, I GUESS. SOUTH OF SOME. AND NORTH.
HMPH.
GOOD ANSWER.
USED TO KNOW THESE WATERS LIKE THE TATTOOS ON MY SON'S FACE.
KNEW WHERE THE FISH WERE WHICH MONTH OF THE YEAR, WHAT TIME OF DAY THEY LIKED TO BITE BEST...
USED T'BE ENOUGH IN THIS LAGOON TO SELL TO THE TOURISTS.
THEN AT LEAST ENOUGH FOR THE WHOLE VILLAGE. ENOUGH TO FEED MY FAMILY... NOW T'AIN'T HARDLY ENOUGH TO KEEP THE MEAT ON THESE SKINNY BONES!
RRGL
HEY!
SQRRM
AGH!!! YOU TALKED!
I KNOW AN OLD MAN COMES ON TO RAMBLING, SON... BUT WE JUST MET NOT A FEW MINUTES AGO!

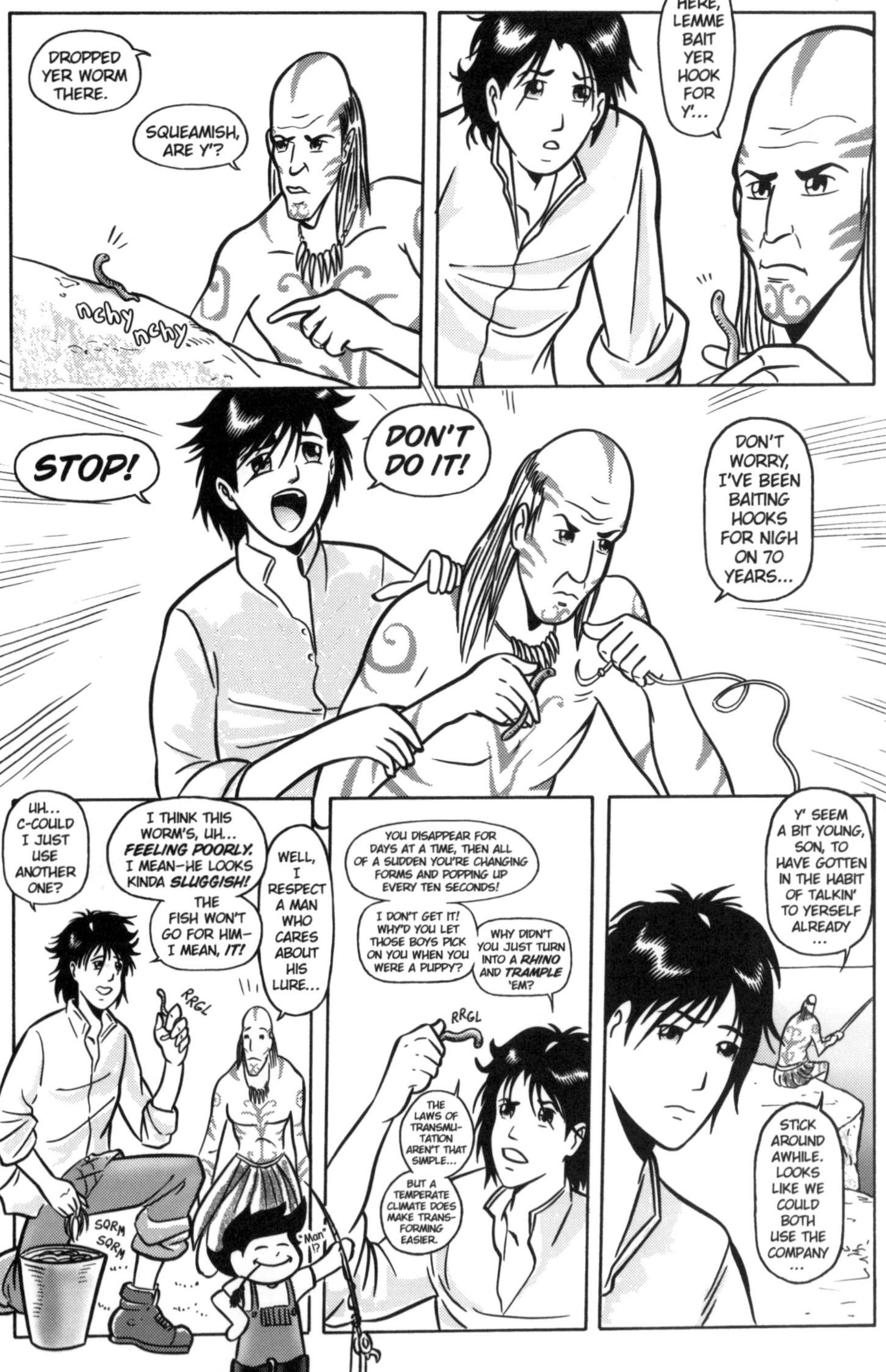
DROPPED YER WORM THERE.
SQUEAMISH, ARE Y'?
nchy nchy
HERE, LEMME BAIT YER HOOK FOR Y'...
STOP!
DON'T DO IT!
DON'T WORRY, I'VE BEEN BAITING HOOKS FOR NIGH ON 70 YEARS...
UH... C-COULD I JUST USE ANOTHER ONE?
I THINK THIS WORM'S, UH... **FEELING POORLY.** I MEAN—HE LOOKS KINDA **SLUGGISH!**
THE FISH WON'T GO FOR HIM— I MEAN, **IT!**
WELL, I RESPECT A MAN WHO CARES ABOUT HIS LURE...
RRGL
SQRM SQRM
"Man" !?
YOU DISAPPEAR FOR DAYS AT A TIME, THEN ALL OF A SUDDEN YOU'RE CHANGING FORMS AND POPPING UP EVERY TEN SECONDS!
I DON'T GET IT! WHY'D YOU LET THOSE BOYS PICK ON YOU WHEN YOU WERE A PUPPY?
WHY DIDN'T YOU JUST TURN INTO A **RHINO** AND **TRAMPLE** 'EM?
RRGL
THE LAWS OF TRANSMUTATION AREN'T THAT SIMPLE...
BUT A TEMPERATE CLIMATE DOES MAKE TRANSFORMING EASIER.
Y' SEEM A BIT YOUNG, SON, TO HAVE GOTTEN IN THE HABIT OF TALKIN' TO YERSELF ALREADY ...
STICK AROUND AWHILE. LOOKS LIKE WE COULD BOTH USE THE COMPANY ...

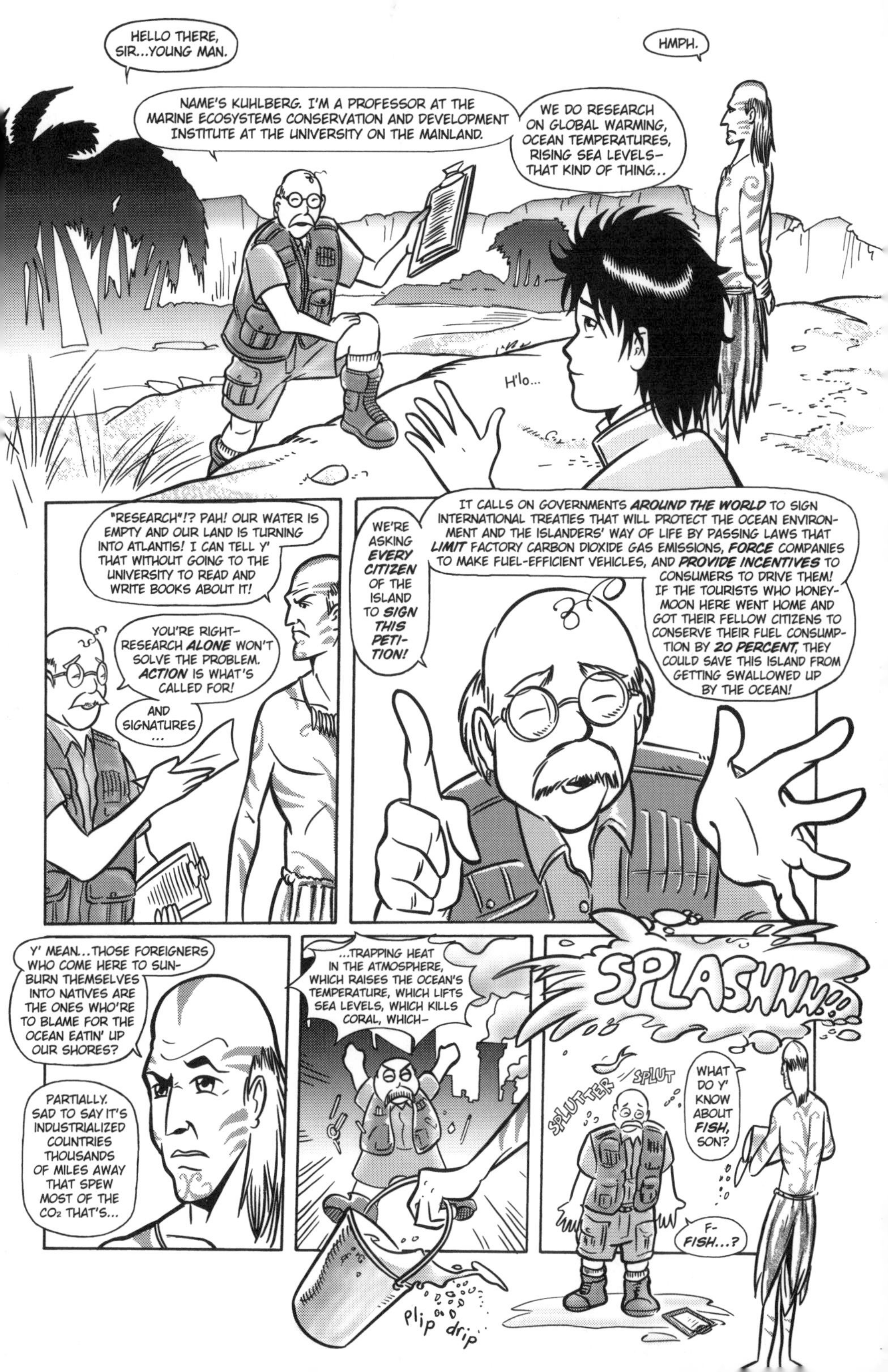
HELLO THERE, SIR...YOUNG MAN.
HMPH.
NAME'S KUHLBERG. I'M A PROFESSOR AT THE MARINE ECOSYSTEMS CONSERVATION AND DEVELOPMENT INSTITUTE AT THE UNIVERSITY ON THE MAINLAND.
WE DO RESEARCH ON GLOBAL WARMING, OCEAN TEMPERATURES, RISING SEA LEVELS– THAT KIND OF THING...
H'lo...
"RESEARCH"!? PAH! OUR WATER IS EMPTY AND OUR LAND IS TURNING INTO ATLANTIS! I CAN TELL Y' THAT WITHOUT GOING TO THE UNIVERSITY TO READ AND WRITE BOOKS ABOUT IT!
YOU'RE RIGHT– RESEARCH ALONE WON'T SOLVE THE PROBLEM. ACTION IS WHAT'S CALLED FOR!
AND SIGNATURES...
WE'RE ASKING EVERY CITIZEN OF THE ISLAND TO SIGN THIS PETITION!
IT CALLS ON GOVERNMENTS AROUND THE WORLD TO SIGN INTERNATIONAL TREATIES THAT WILL PROTECT THE OCEAN ENVIRONMENT AND THE ISLANDERS' WAY OF LIFE BY PASSING LAWS THAT LIMIT FACTORY CARBON DIOXIDE GAS EMISSIONS, FORCE COMPANIES TO MAKE FUEL-EFFICIENT VEHICLES, AND PROVIDE INCENTIVES TO CONSUMERS TO DRIVE THEM! IF THE TOURISTS WHO HONEYMOON HERE WENT HOME AND GOT THEIR FELLOW CITIZENS TO CONSERVE THEIR FUEL CONSUMPTION BY 20 PERCENT, THEY COULD SAVE THIS ISLAND FROM GETTING SWALLOWED UP BY THE OCEAN!
Y' MEAN...THOSE FOREIGNERS WHO COME HERE TO SUNBURN THEMSELVES INTO NATIVES ARE THE ONES WHO'RE TO BLAME FOR THE OCEAN EATIN' UP OUR SHORES?
PARTIALLY. SAD TO SAY IT'S INDUSTRIALIZED COUNTRIES THOUSANDS OF MILES AWAY THAT SPEW MOST OF THE CO2 THAT'S...
...TRAPPING HEAT IN THE ATMOSPHERE, WHICH RAISES THE OCEAN'S TEMPERATURE, WHICH LIFTS SEA LEVELS, WHICH KILLS CORAL, WHICH–
plip drip
SPLASHHH!?!
SPLUTTER SPLUT
WHAT DO Y' KNOW ABOUT FISH, SON?
F- FISH...?

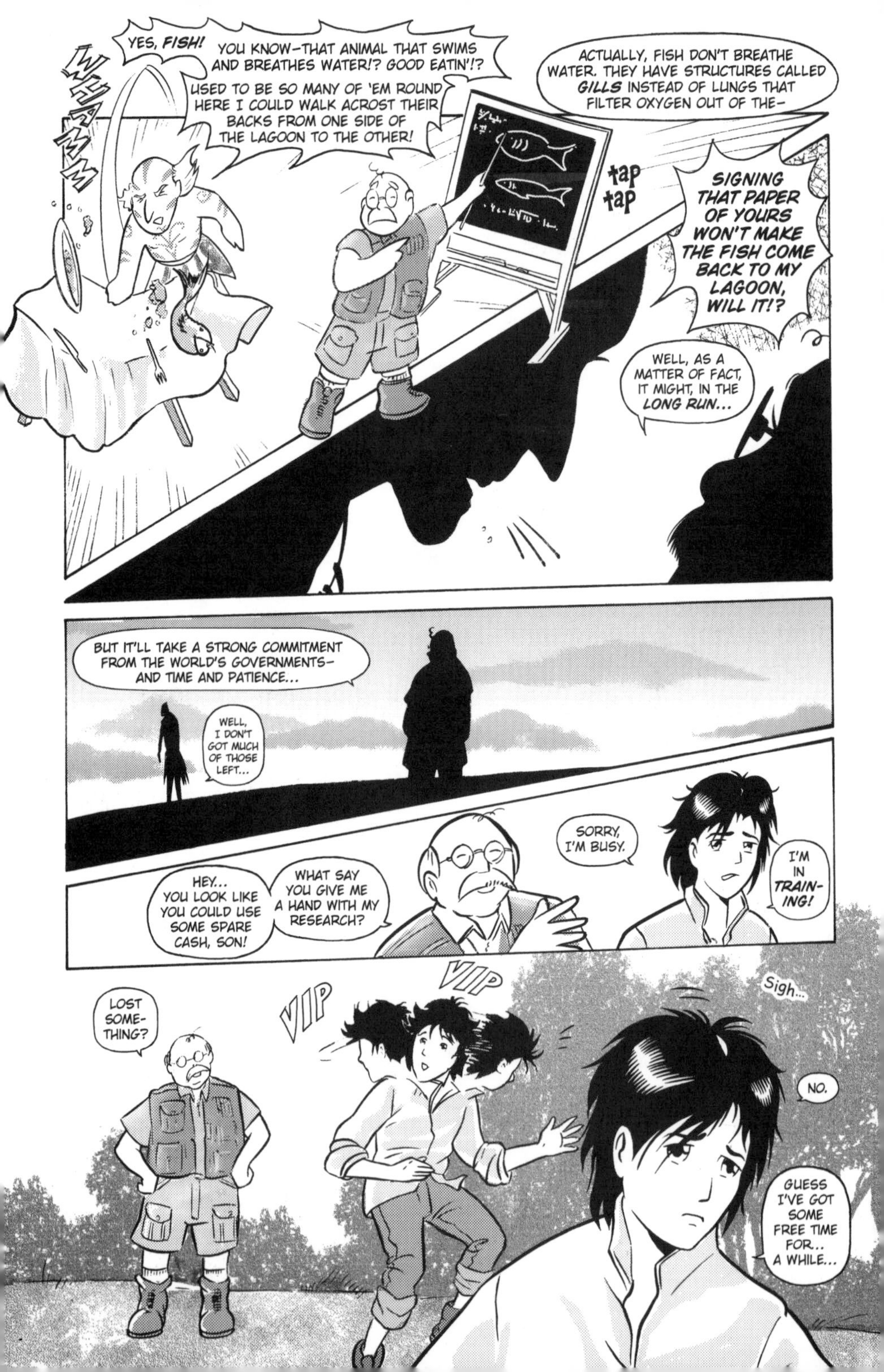
WHAMMM
YES, FISH!
YOU KNOW—THAT ANIMAL THAT SWIMS AND BREATHES WATER!? GOOD EATIN'!?
USED TO BE SO MANY OF 'EM ROUND HERE I COULD WALK ACROST THEIR BACKS FROM ONE SIDE OF THE LAGOON TO THE OTHER!
ACTUALLY, FISH DON'T BREATHE WATER. THEY HAVE STRUCTURES CALLED GILLS INSTEAD OF LUNGS THAT FILTER OXYGEN OUT OF THE—
tap tap
SIGNING THAT PAPER OF YOURS WON'T MAKE THE FISH COME BACK TO MY LAGOON, WILL IT!?
WELL, AS A MATTER OF FACT, IT MIGHT, IN THE LONG RUN...
BUT IT'LL TAKE A STRONG COMMITMENT FROM THE WORLD'S GOVERNMENTS— AND TIME AND PATIENCE...
WELL, I DON'T GOT MUCH OF THOSE LEFT...
HEY... YOU LOOK LIKE YOU COULD USE SOME SPARE CASH, SON!
WHAT SAY YOU GIVE ME A HAND WITH MY RESEARCH?
SORRY, I'M BUSY.
I'M IN TRAIN-ING!
LOST SOME-THING?
VIP
VIP
Sigh...
NO.
GUESS I'VE GOT SOME FREE TIME FOR... A WHILE...

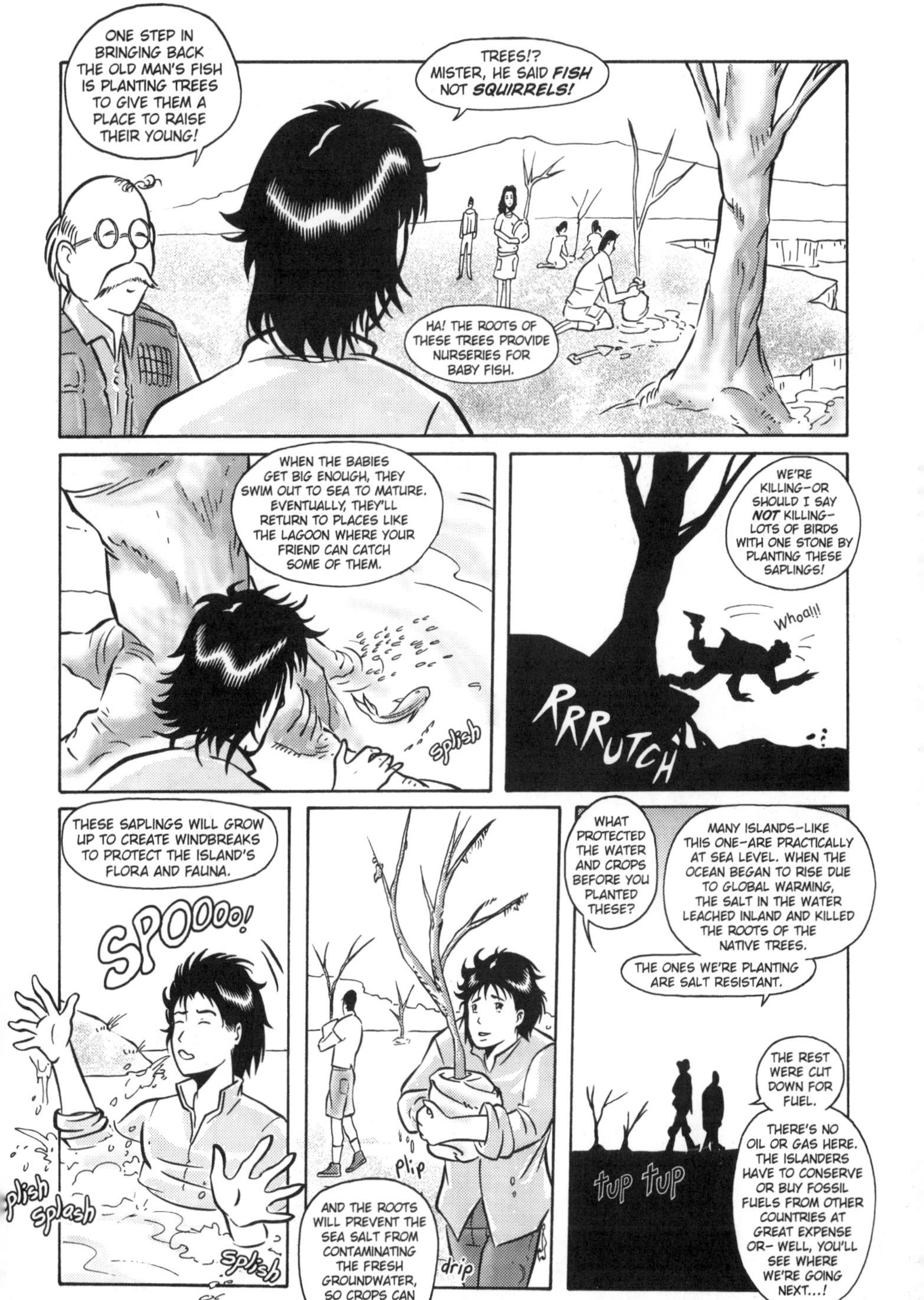
ONE STEP IN BRINGING BACK THE OLD MAN'S FISH IS PLANTING TREES TO GIVE THEM A PLACE TO RAISE THEIR YOUNG!
TREES!? MISTER, HE SAID *FISH* NOT *SQUIRRELS!*
HA! THE ROOTS OF THESE TREES PROVIDE NURSERIES FOR BABY FISH.
WHEN THE BABIES GET BIG ENOUGH, THEY SWIM OUT TO SEA TO MATURE. EVENTUALLY, THEY'LL RETURN TO PLACES LIKE THE LAGOON WHERE YOUR FRIEND CAN CATCH SOME OF THEM.
splish
WE'RE KILLING—OR SHOULD I SAY *NOT* KILLING—LOTS OF BIRDS WITH ONE STONE BY PLANTING THESE SAPLINGS!
Whoa!!!
RRRUTCH
THESE SAPLINGS WILL GROW UP TO CREATE WINDBREAKS TO PROTECT THE ISLAND'S FLORA AND FAUNA.
SPOOooo!
plish
splash
splish
plip
AND THE ROOTS WILL PREVENT THE SEA SALT FROM CONTAMINATING THE FRESH GROUNDWATER, SO CROPS CAN GROW INLAND.
drip
WHAT PROTECTED THE WATER AND CROPS BEFORE YOU PLANTED THESE?
MANY ISLANDS—LIKE THIS ONE—ARE PRACTICALLY AT SEA LEVEL. WHEN THE OCEAN BEGAN TO RISE DUE TO GLOBAL WARMING, THE SALT IN THE WATER LEACHED INLAND AND KILLED THE ROOTS OF THE NATIVE TREES.
THE ONES WE'RE PLANTING ARE SALT RESISTANT.
THE REST WERE CUT DOWN FOR FUEL.
THERE'S NO OIL OR GAS HERE. THE ISLANDERS HAVE TO CONSERVE OR BUY FOSSIL FUELS FROM OTHER COUNTRIES AT GREAT EXPENSE OR— WELL, YOU'LL SEE WHERE WE'RE GOING NEXT...!
tup tup

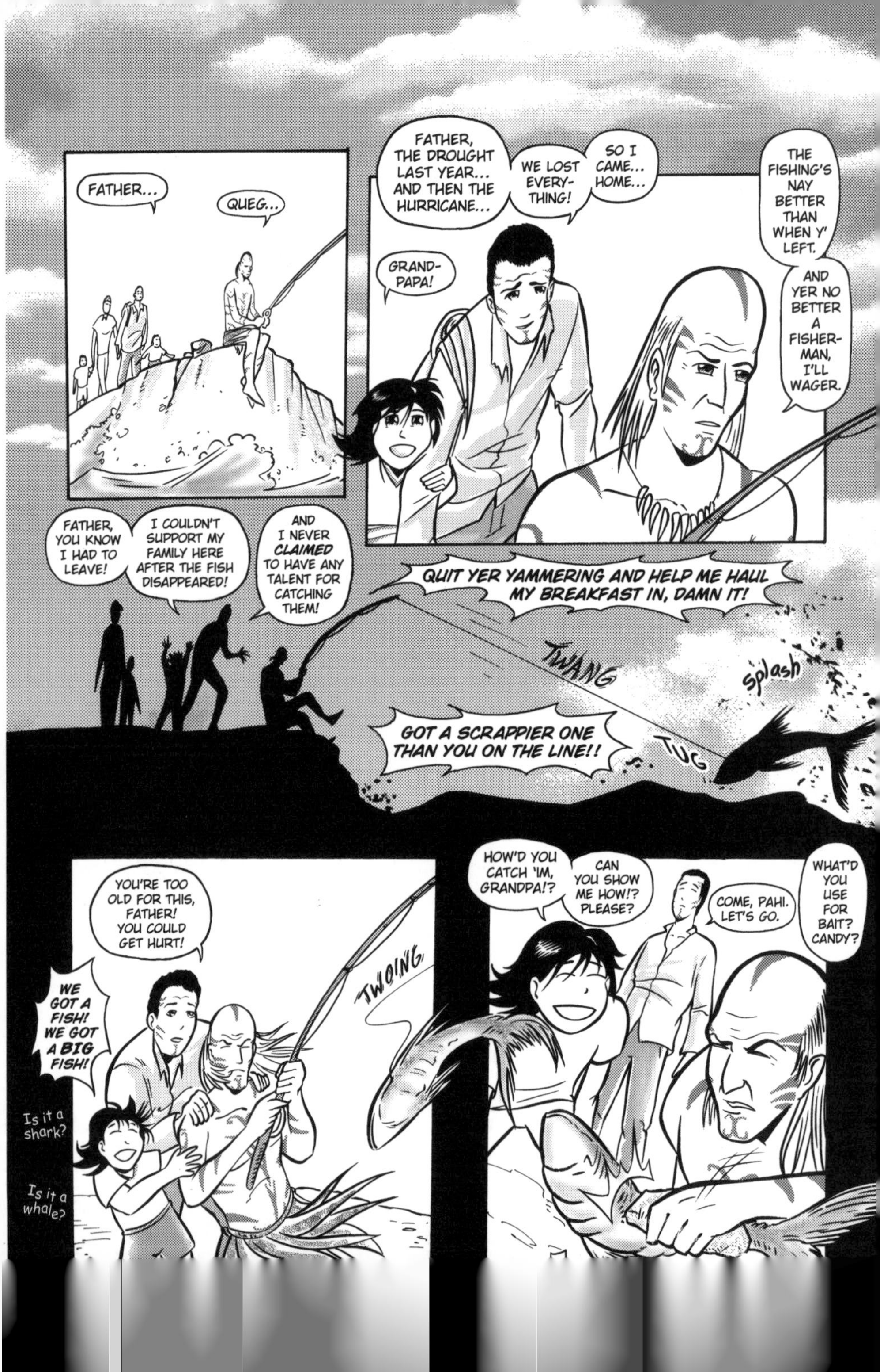
FATHER...
QUEG...
FATHER, THE DROUGHT LAST YEAR... AND THEN THE HURRICANE...
WE LOST EVERY-THING!
SO I CAME... HOME...
GRAND-PAPA!
THE FISHING'S NAY BETTER THAN WHEN Y' LEFT.
AND YER NO BETTER A FISHER-MAN, I'LL WAGER.
FATHER, YOU KNOW I HAD TO LEAVE!
I COULDN'T SUPPORT MY FAMILY HERE AFTER THE FISH DISAPPEARED!
AND I NEVER CLAIMED TO HAVE ANY TALENT FOR CATCHING THEM!
QUIT YER YAMMERING AND HELP ME HAUL MY BREAKFAST IN, DAMN IT!
TWANG
Splash
GOT A SCRAPPIER ONE THAN YOU ON THE LINE!!
TUG
YOU'RE TOO OLD FOR THIS, FATHER! YOU COULD GET HURT!
WE GOT A FISH! WE GOT A BIG FISH!
TWOING
Is it a shark?
Is it a whale?
HOW'D YOU CATCH 'IM, GRANDPA!?
CAN YOU SHOW ME HOW!? PLEASE?
COME, PAHI. LET'S GO.
WHAT'D YOU USE FOR BAIT? CANDY?

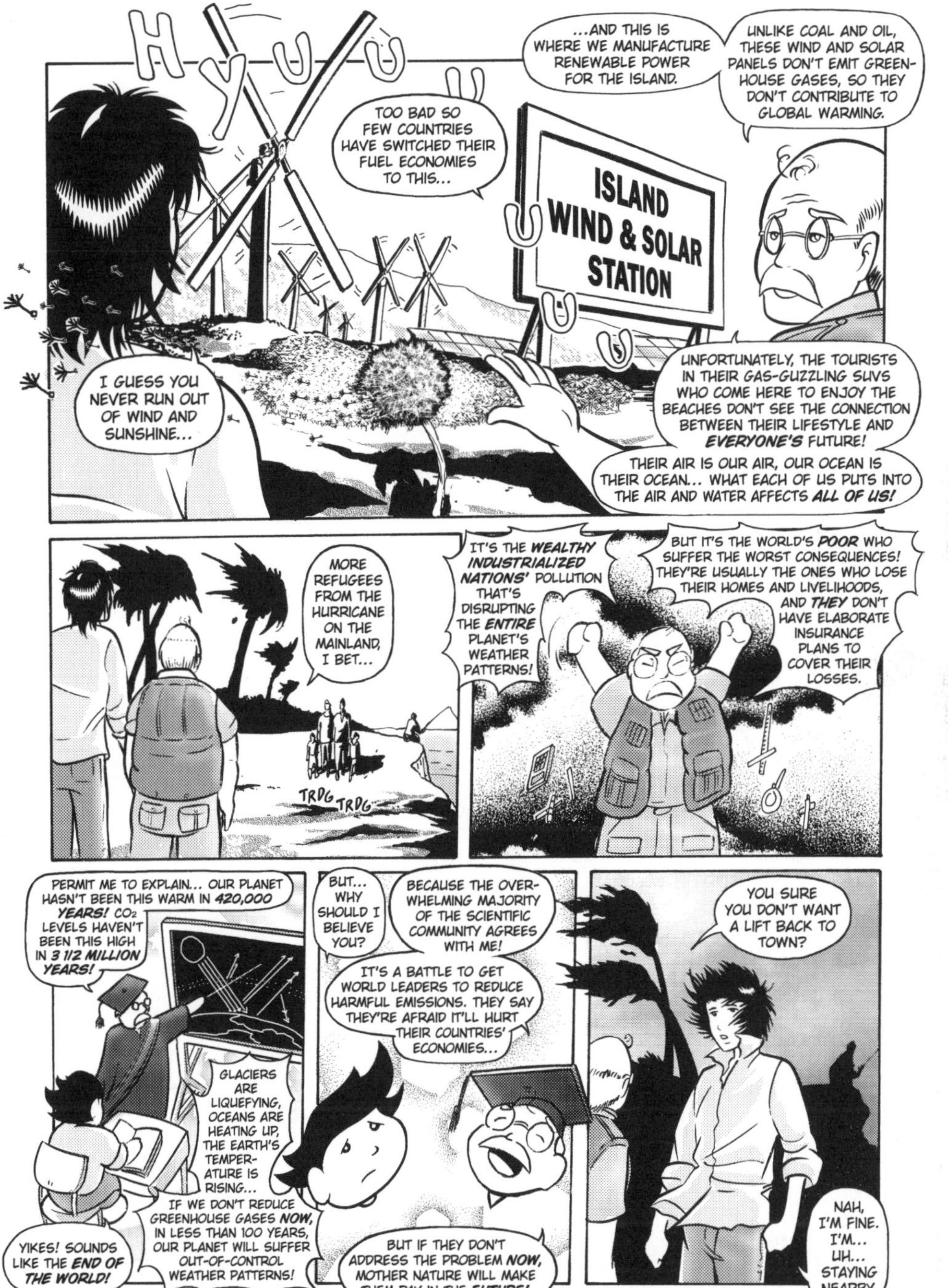
HYUUUUUUU
TOO BAD SO FEW COUNTRIES HAVE SWITCHED THEIR FUEL ECONOMIES TO THIS...
ISLAND WIND & SOLAR STATION
...AND THIS IS WHERE WE MANUFACTURE RENEWABLE POWER FOR THE ISLAND.
UNLIKE COAL AND OIL, THESE WIND AND SOLAR PANELS DON'T EMIT GREEN-HOUSE GASES, SO THEY DON'T CONTRIBUTE TO GLOBAL WARMING.
I GUESS YOU NEVER RUN OUT OF WIND AND SUNSHINE...
UNFORTUNATELY, THE TOURISTS IN THEIR GAS-GUZZLING SUVS WHO COME HERE TO ENJOY THE BEACHES DON'T SEE THE CONNECTION BETWEEN THEIR LIFESTYLE AND EVERYONE'S FUTURE!
THEIR AIR IS OUR AIR, OUR OCEAN IS THEIR OCEAN... WHAT EACH OF US PUTS INTO THE AIR AND WATER AFFECTS ALL OF US!
MORE REFUGEES FROM THE HURRICANE ON THE MAINLAND, I BET...
TRDG TRDG
IT'S THE WEALTHY INDUSTRIALIZED NATIONS' POLLUTION THAT'S DISRUPTING THE ENTIRE PLANET'S WEATHER PATTERNS!
BUT IT'S THE WORLD'S POOR WHO SUFFER THE WORST CONSEQUENCES! THEY'RE USUALLY THE ONES WHO LOSE THEIR HOMES AND LIVELIHOODS, AND THEY DON'T HAVE ELABORATE INSURANCE PLANS TO COVER THEIR LOSSES.
PERMIT ME TO EXPLAIN... OUR PLANET HASN'T BEEN THIS WARM IN 420,000 YEARS! CO_2 LEVELS HAVEN'T BEEN THIS HIGH IN 3 1/2 MILLION YEARS!
GLACIERS ARE LIQUEFYING, OCEANS ARE HEATING UP, THE EARTH'S TEMPER-ATURE IS RISING...
IF WE DON'T REDUCE GREENHOUSE GASES NOW, IN LESS THAN 100 YEARS, OUR PLANET WILL SUFFER OUT-OF-CONTROL WEATHER PATTERNS!
YIKES! SOUNDS LIKE THE END OF THE WORLD!
Hurricanes! Floods! Droughts!
BUT... WHY SHOULD I BELIEVE YOU?
BECAUSE THE OVER-WHELMING MAJORITY OF THE SCIENTIFIC COMMUNITY AGREES WITH ME!
IT'S A BATTLE TO GET WORLD LEADERS TO REDUCE HARMFUL EMISSIONS. THEY SAY THEY'RE AFRAID IT'LL HURT THEIR COUNTRIES' ECONOMIES...
BUT IF THEY DON'T ADDRESS THE PROBLEM NOW, MOTHER NATURE WILL MAKE THEM PAY IN THE FUTURE!
YOU SURE YOU DON'T WANT A LIFT BACK TO TOWN?
NAH, I'M FINE. I'M... UH... STAYING NEARBY.

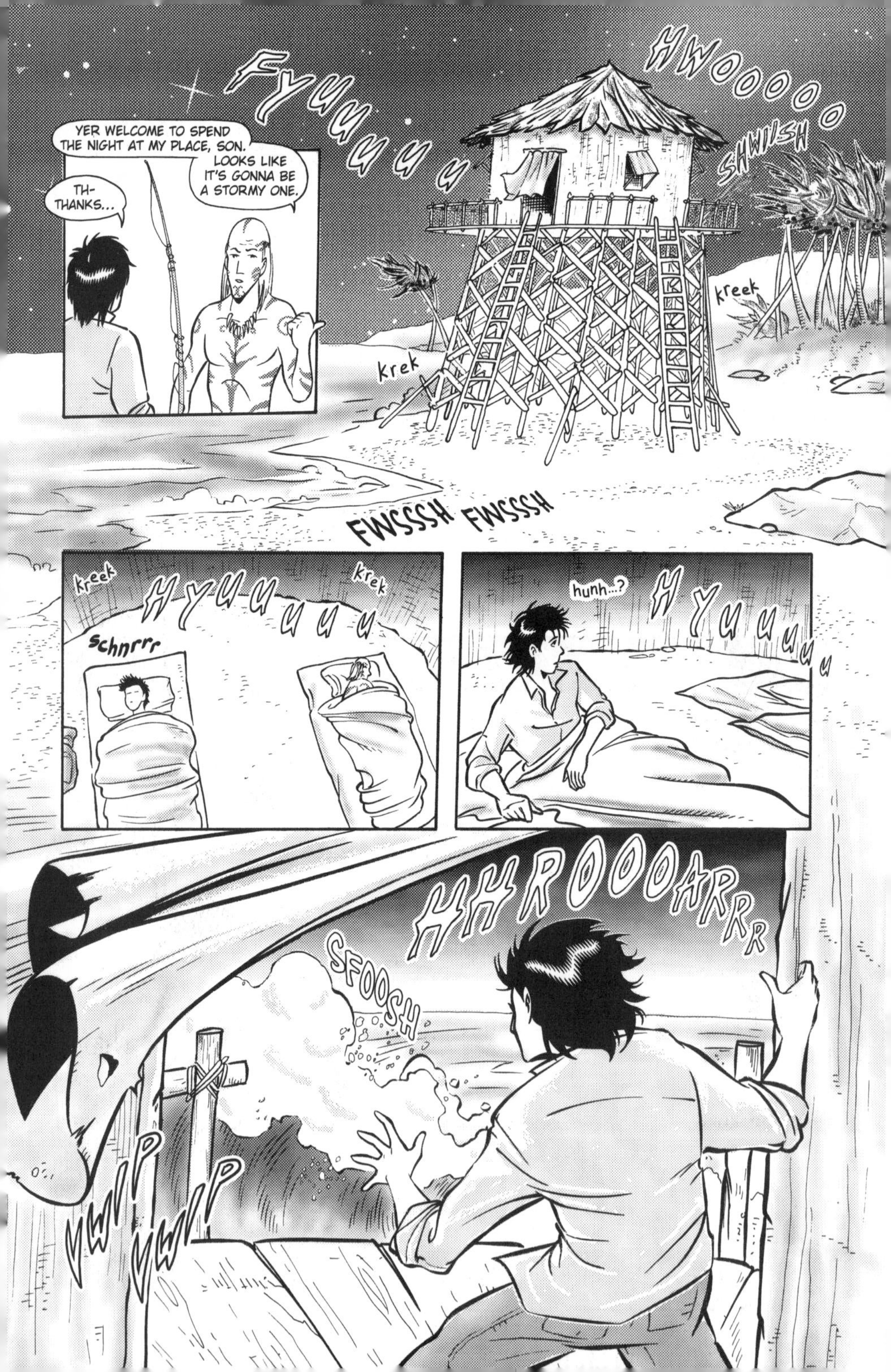
FYUUUUUU
HWOOOOOO
SHWIISH
YER WELCOME TO SPEND THE NIGHT AT MY PLACE, SON.
LOOKS LIKE IT'S GONNA BE A STORMY ONE.
TH-THANKS...
kreek
krek
FWSSSH FWSSSH
kreek
HYUUUUUU
krek
schnrrr
hunh...?
HYUUUUUU
HHROOOARRR
SFOOSH
VWIP VWIP

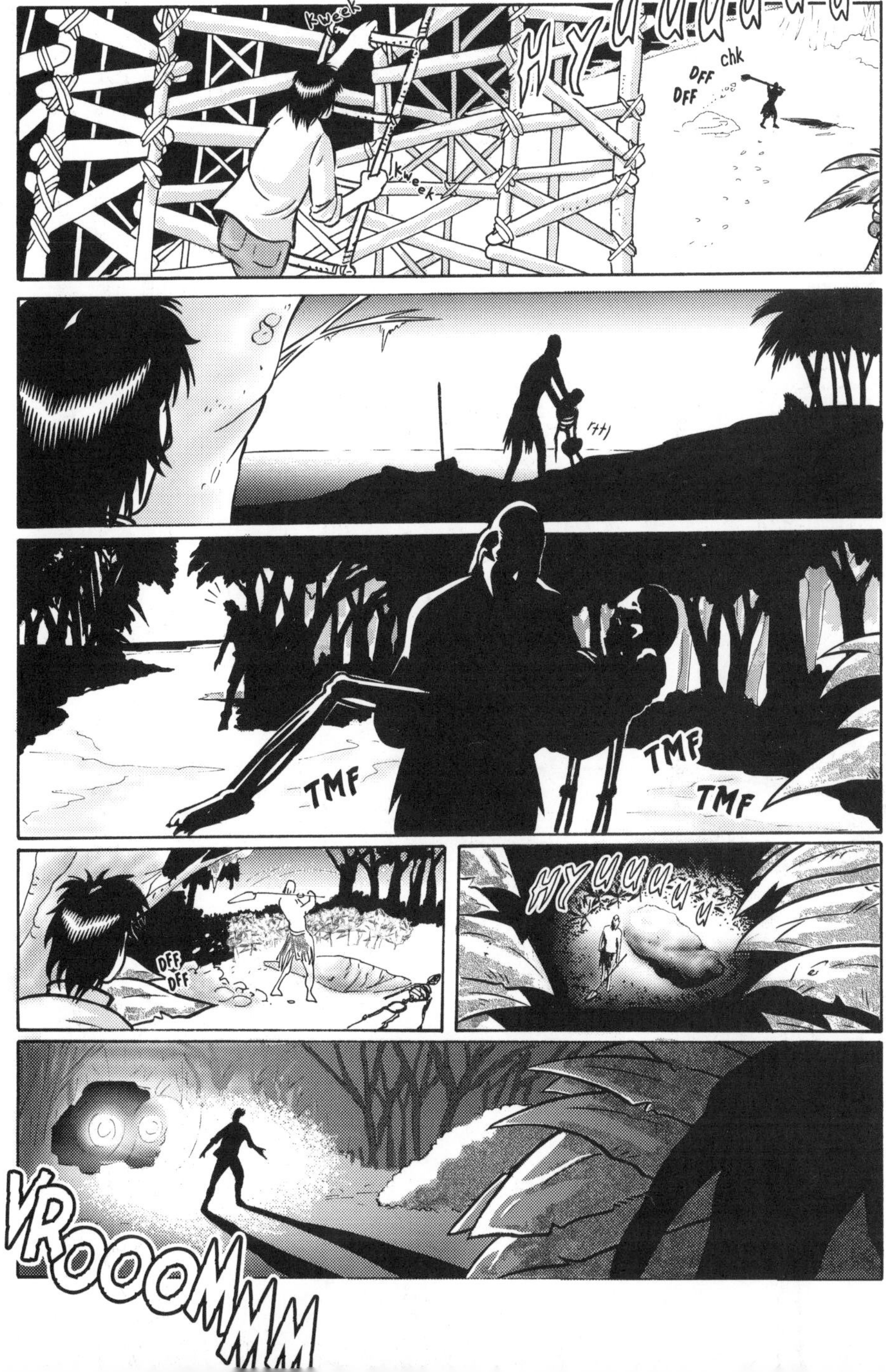
Kweek
Kweek
HYU-U-U-U-U-U-U
chk
DFF
DFF
TMF
TMF
TMF
DFF
DFF
HYUUUUUU
VROOOMMMM

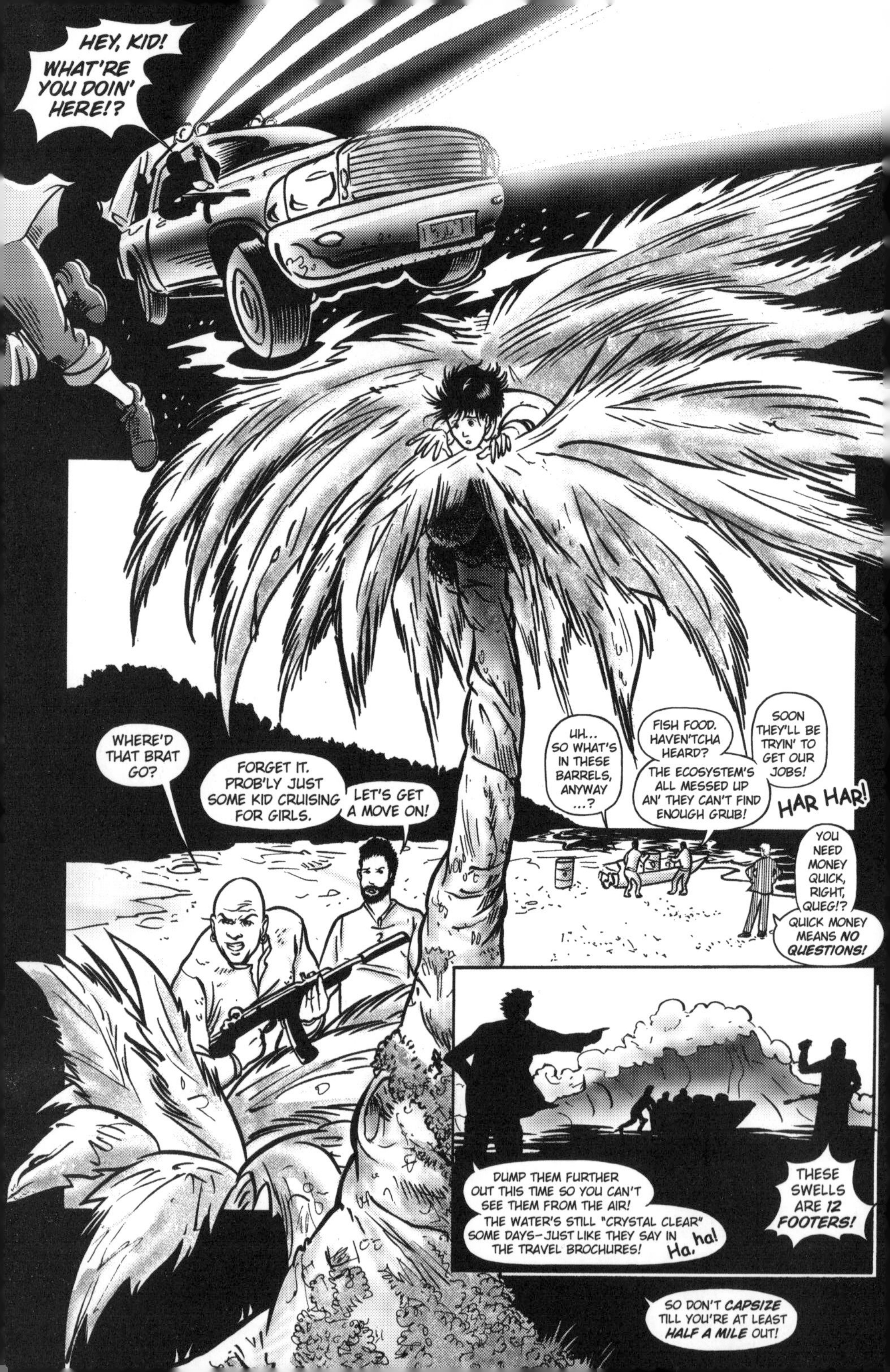
HEY, KID! WHAT'RE YOU DOIN' HERE!?
WHERE'D THAT BRAT GO?
FORGET IT. PROB'LY JUST SOME KID CRUISING FOR GIRLS.
LET'S GET A MOVE ON!
UH... SO WHAT'S IN THESE BARRELS, ANYWAY ...?
FISH FOOD. HAVEN'TCHA HEARD?
THE ECOSYSTEM'S ALL MESSED UP AN' THEY CAN'T FIND ENOUGH GRUB!
SOON THEY'LL BE TRYIN' TO GET OUR JOBS!
HAR HAR!
YOU NEED MONEY QUICK, RIGHT, QUEG!?
QUICK MONEY MEANS NO QUESTIONS!
DUMP THEM FURTHER OUT THIS TIME SO YOU CAN'T SEE THEM FROM THE AIR!
THE WATER'S STILL "CRYSTAL CLEAR" SOME DAYS—JUST LIKE THEY SAY IN THE TRAVEL BROCHURES!
Ha, ha!
THESE SWELLS ARE 12 FOOTERS!
SO DON'T CAPSIZE TILL YOU'RE AT LEAST HALF A MILE OUT!

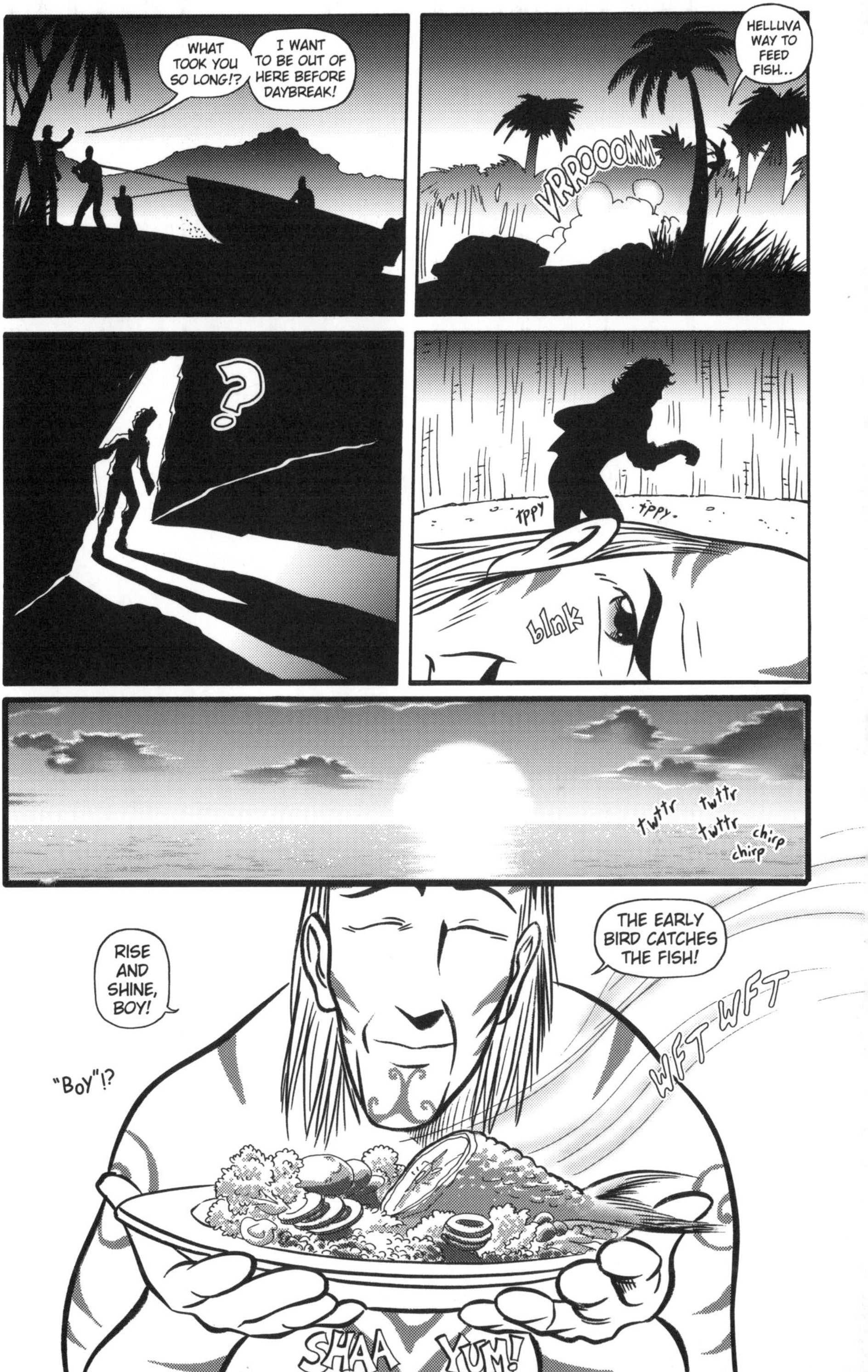
WHAT TOOK YOU SO LONG!?
I WANT TO BE OUT OF HERE BEFORE DAYBREAK!
HELLUVA WAY TO FEED FISH...
VRROOOMM
?
tppy
tppy
blnk
twttr twttr
twttr
chirp chirp
RISE AND SHINE, BOY!
THE EARLY BIRD CATCHES THE FISH!
WFT WFT
"BOY"!?
SHAA YUM!

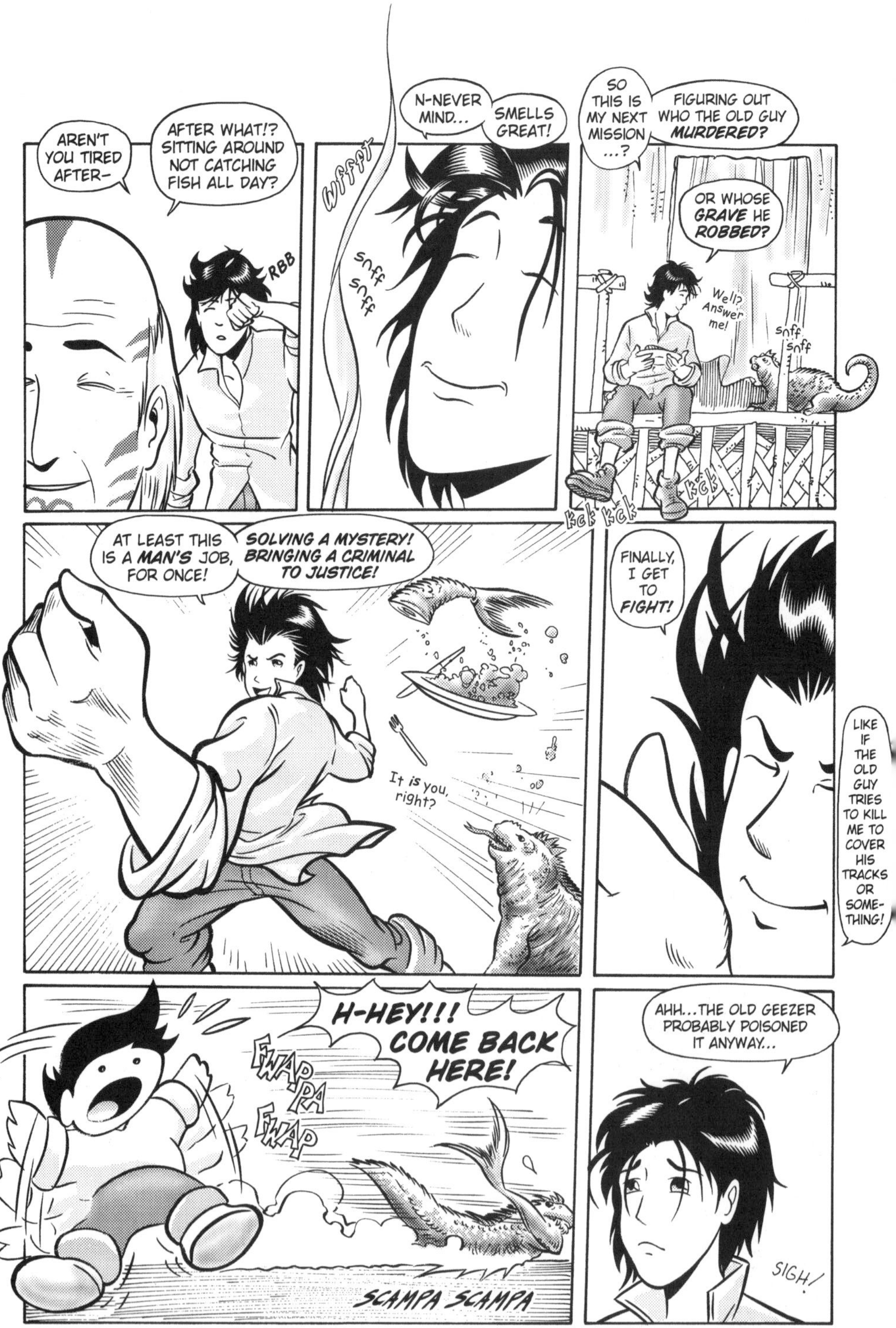
AREN'T YOU TIRED AFTER–
AFTER WHAT!? SITTING AROUND NOT CATCHING FISH ALL DAY?
RBB
wffft
N-NEVER MIND...
SMELLS GREAT!
snff snff
SO THIS IS MY NEXT MISSION ...?
FIGURING OUT WHO THE OLD GUY MURDERED?
OR WHOSE GRAVE HE ROBBED?
Well? Answer me!
snff snff
kck kck kck
AT LEAST THIS IS A MAN'S JOB, FOR ONCE!
SOLVING A MYSTERY! BRINGING A CRIMINAL TO JUSTICE!
It is you, right?
FINALLY, I GET TO FIGHT!
LIKE IF THE OLD GUY TRIES TO KILL ME TO COVER HIS TRACKS OR SOME-THING!
H-HEY!!! COME BACK HERE!
FWAPPA FWAP
SCAMPA SCAMPA
AHH...THE OLD GEEZER PROBABLY POISONED IT ANYWAY...
SIGH!

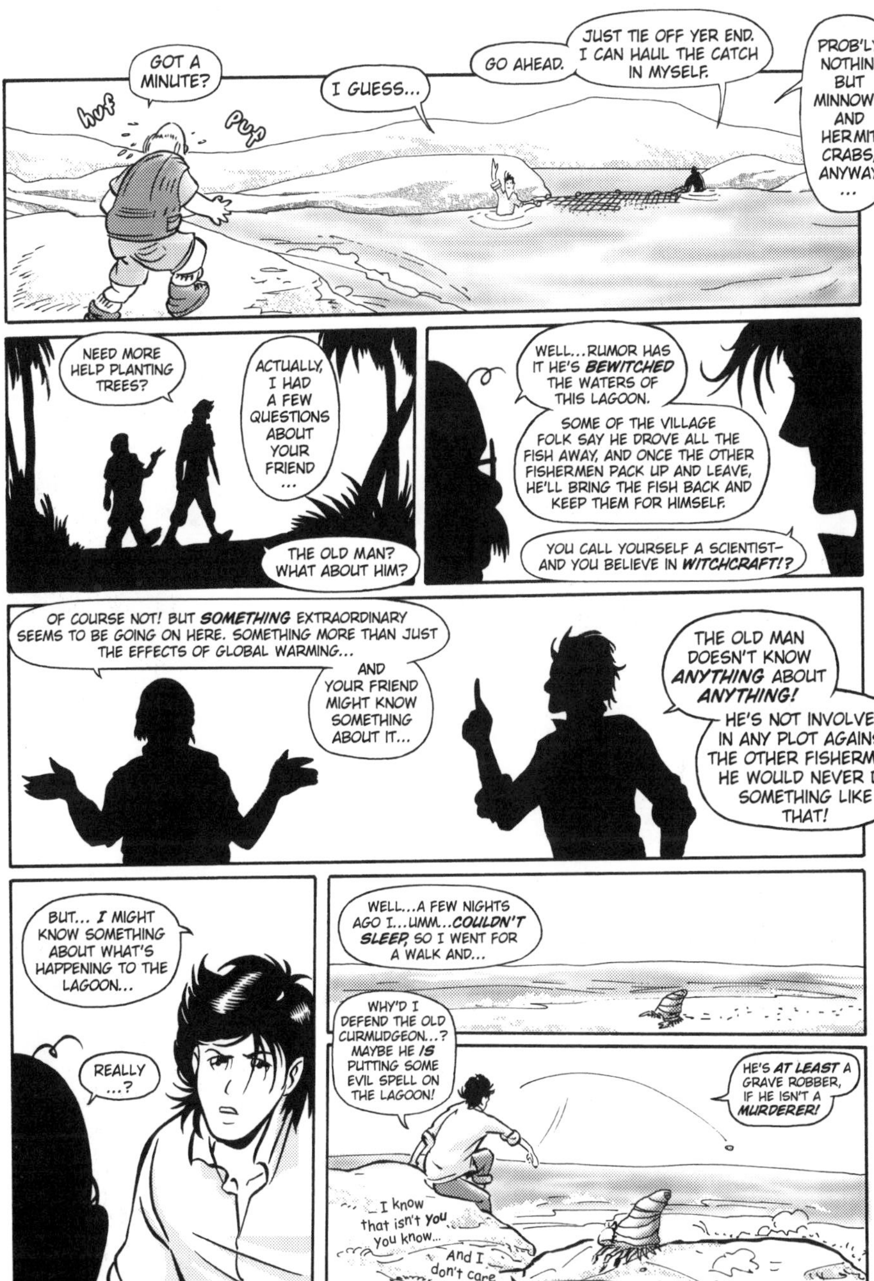

huf
GOT A MINUTE?
Pup
I GUESS...
GO AHEAD.
JUST TIE OFF YER END. I CAN HAUL THE CATCH IN MYSELF.
PROB'LY NOTHIN' BUT MINNOWS AND HERMIT CRABS, ANYWAY ...
NEED MORE HELP PLANTING TREES?
ACTUALLY, I HAD A FEW QUESTIONS ABOUT YOUR FRIEND ...
THE OLD MAN? WHAT ABOUT HIM?
WELL...RUMOR HAS IT HE'S BEWITCHED THE WATERS OF THIS LAGOON.
SOME OF THE VILLAGE FOLK SAY HE DROVE ALL THE FISH AWAY, AND ONCE THE OTHER FISHERMEN PACK UP AND LEAVE, HE'LL BRING THE FISH BACK AND KEEP THEM FOR HIMSELF.
YOU CALL YOURSELF A SCIENTIST– AND YOU BELIEVE IN WITCHCRAFT!?
OF COURSE NOT! BUT SOMETHING EXTRAORDINARY SEEMS TO BE GOING ON HERE. SOMETHING MORE THAN JUST THE EFFECTS OF GLOBAL WARMING...
AND YOUR FRIEND MIGHT KNOW SOMETHING ABOUT IT...
THE OLD MAN DOESN'T KNOW ANYTHING ABOUT ANYTHING!
HE'S NOT INVOLVED IN ANY PLOT AGAINST THE OTHER FISHERMEN! HE WOULD NEVER DO SOMETHING LIKE THAT!
BUT... I MIGHT KNOW SOMETHING ABOUT WHAT'S HAPPENING TO THE LAGOON...
REALLY ...?
WELL...A FEW NIGHTS AGO I...UMM...COULDN'T SLEEP, SO I WENT FOR A WALK AND...
WHY'D I DEFEND THE OLD CURMUDGEON...? MAYBE HE IS PUTTING SOME EVIL SPELL ON THE LAGOON!
HE'S AT LEAST A GRAVE ROBBER, IF HE ISN'T A MURDERER!
I know that isn't you you know...
And I don't care if it is or not!
STILL... HE'S BEEN GIVING ME A PLACE TO SLEEP... AND BREAKFAST...
EVEN IF IT IS POISONED...
SOME-TIMES...
MAYBE...

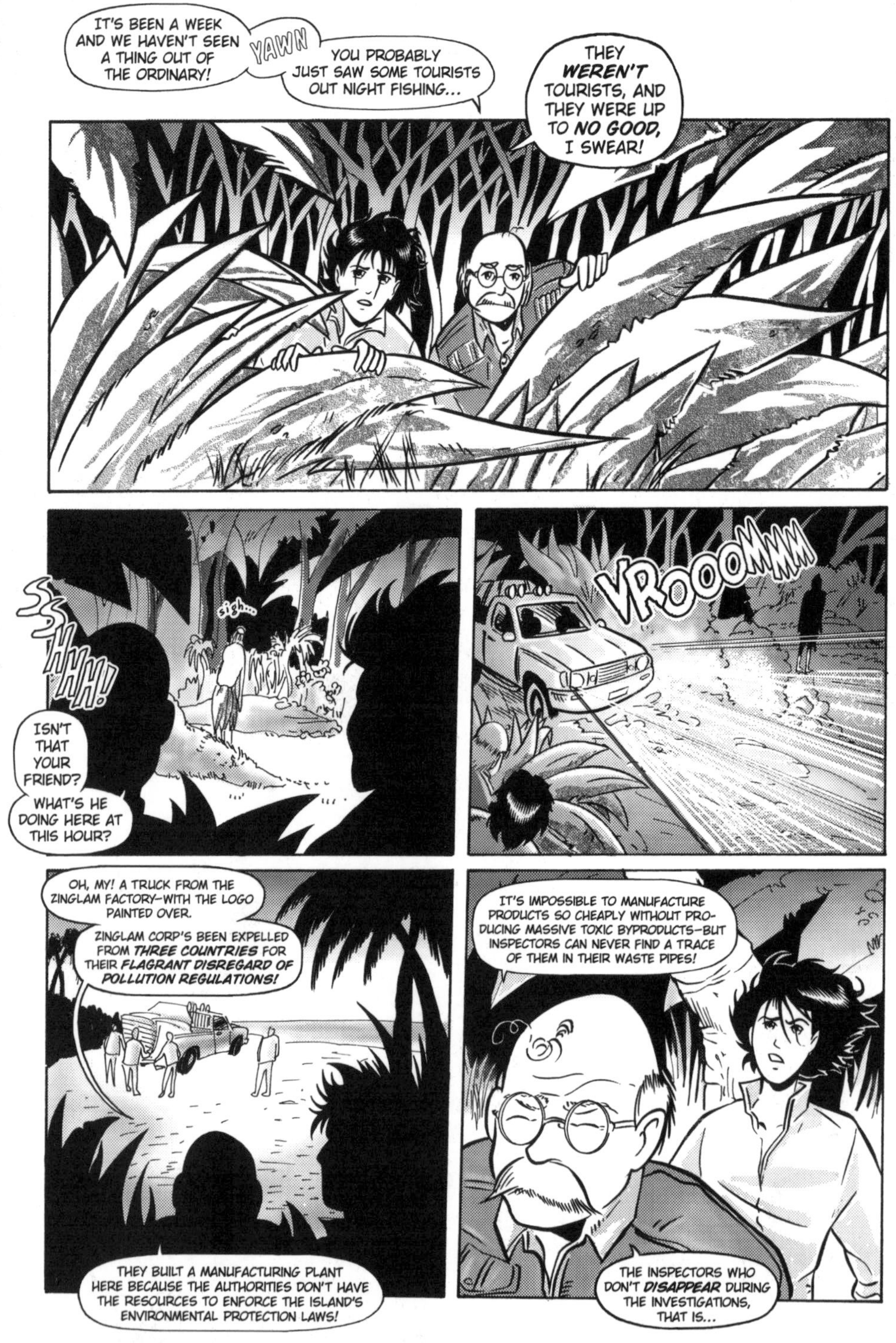
IT'S BEEN A WEEK AND WE HAVEN'T SEEN A THING OUT OF THE ORDINARY!
YAWN
YOU PROBABLY JUST SAW SOME TOURISTS OUT NIGHT FISHING...
THEY **WEREN'T** TOURISTS, AND THEY WERE UP TO **NO GOOD,** I SWEAR!
SSHHH!
sigh...
ISN'T THAT YOUR FRIEND?
WHAT'S HE DOING HERE AT THIS HOUR?
VROOOMMM
OH, MY! A TRUCK FROM THE ZINGLAM FACTORY—WITH THE LOGO PAINTED OVER.
ZINGLAM CORP'S BEEN EXPELLED FROM **THREE COUNTRIES** FOR THEIR **FLAGRANT DISREGARD OF POLLUTION REGULATIONS!**
THEY BUILT A MANUFACTURING PLANT HERE BECAUSE THE AUTHORITIES DON'T HAVE THE RESOURCES TO ENFORCE THE ISLAND'S ENVIRONMENTAL PROTECTION LAWS!
IT'S IMPOSSIBLE TO MANUFACTURE PRODUCTS SO CHEAPLY WITHOUT PRODUCING MASSIVE TOXIC BYPRODUCTS—BUT INSPECTORS CAN NEVER FIND A TRACE OF THEM IN THEIR WASTE PIPES!
THE INSPECTORS WHO DON'T **DISAPPEAR** DURING THE INVESTIGATIONS, THAT IS...

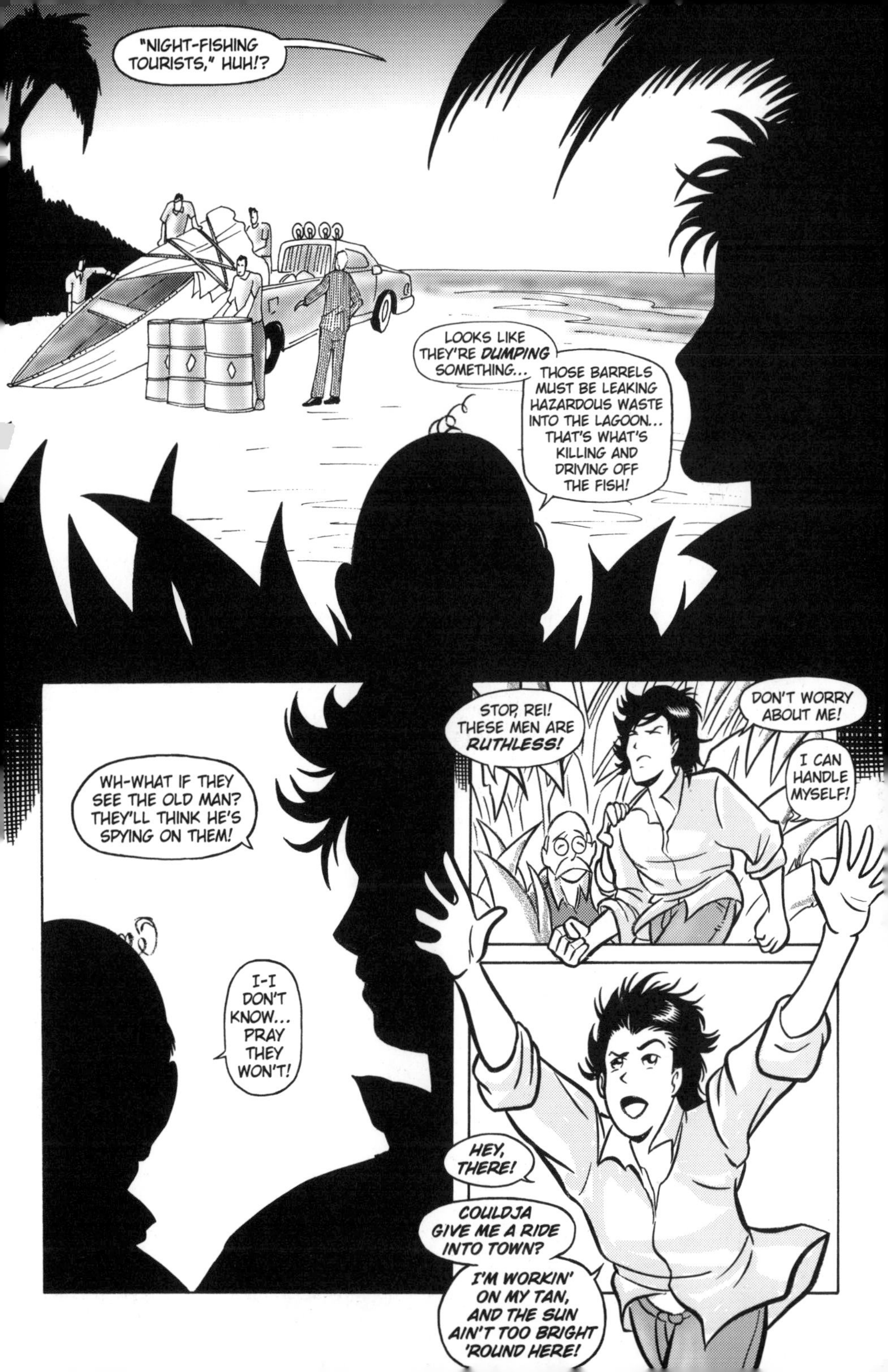
"NIGHT-FISHING TOURISTS," HUH!?
LOOKS LIKE THEY'RE *DUMPING* SOMETHING...
THOSE BARRELS MUST BE LEAKING HAZARDOUS WASTE INTO THE LAGOON... THAT'S WHAT'S KILLING AND DRIVING OFF THE FISH!
WH-WHAT IF THEY SEE THE OLD MAN? THEY'LL THINK HE'S SPYING ON THEM!
I-I DON'T KNOW... PRAY THEY WON'T!
STOP, REI! THESE MEN ARE ***RUTHLESS!***
DON'T WORRY ABOUT ME!
I CAN HANDLE MYSELF!
HEY, THERE!
COULDJA GIVE ME A RIDE INTO TOWN?
I'M WORKIN' ON MY TAN, AND THE SUN AIN'T TOO BRIGHT 'ROUND HERE!

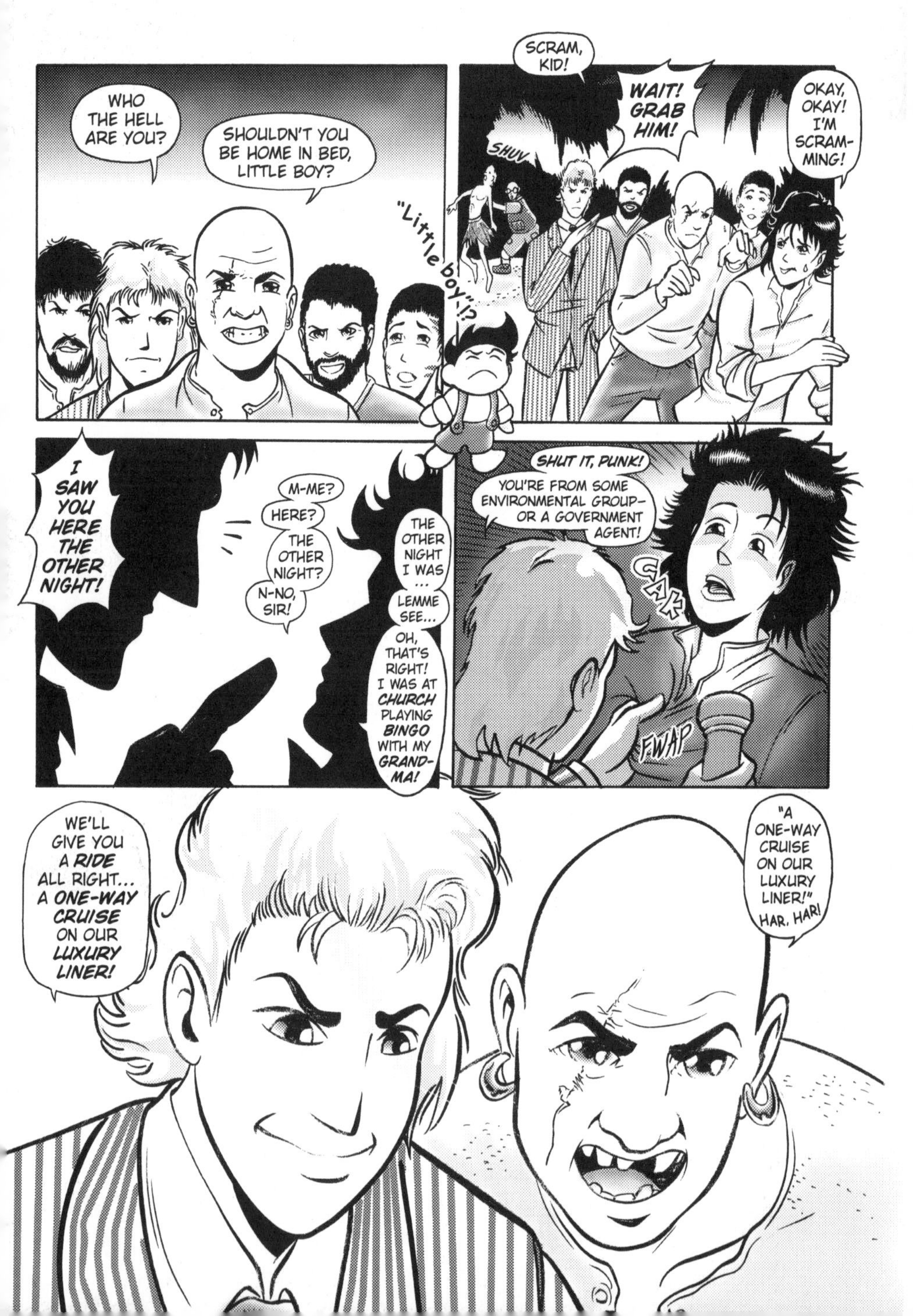
WHO THE HELL ARE YOU?
SHOULDN'T YOU BE HOME IN BED, LITTLE BOY?
"Little boy"!?
SCRAM, KID!
WAIT! GRAB HIM!
OKAY, OKAY! I'M SCRAM-MING!
SHUV
I SAW YOU HERE THE OTHER NIGHT!
M-ME?
HERE?
THE OTHER NIGHT?
N-NO, SIR!
THE OTHER NIGHT I WAS...
LEMME SEE...
OH, THAT'S RIGHT! I WAS AT CHURCH PLAYING BINGO WITH MY GRAND-MA!
SHUT IT, PUNK!
YOU'RE FROM SOME ENVIRONMENTAL GROUP- OR A GOVERNMENT AGENT!
GAK
FWAP
WE'LL GIVE YOU A RIDE ALL RIGHT... A ONE-WAY CRUISE ON OUR LUXURY LINER!
"A ONE-WAY CRUISE ON OUR LUXURY LINER!" HAR, HAR!

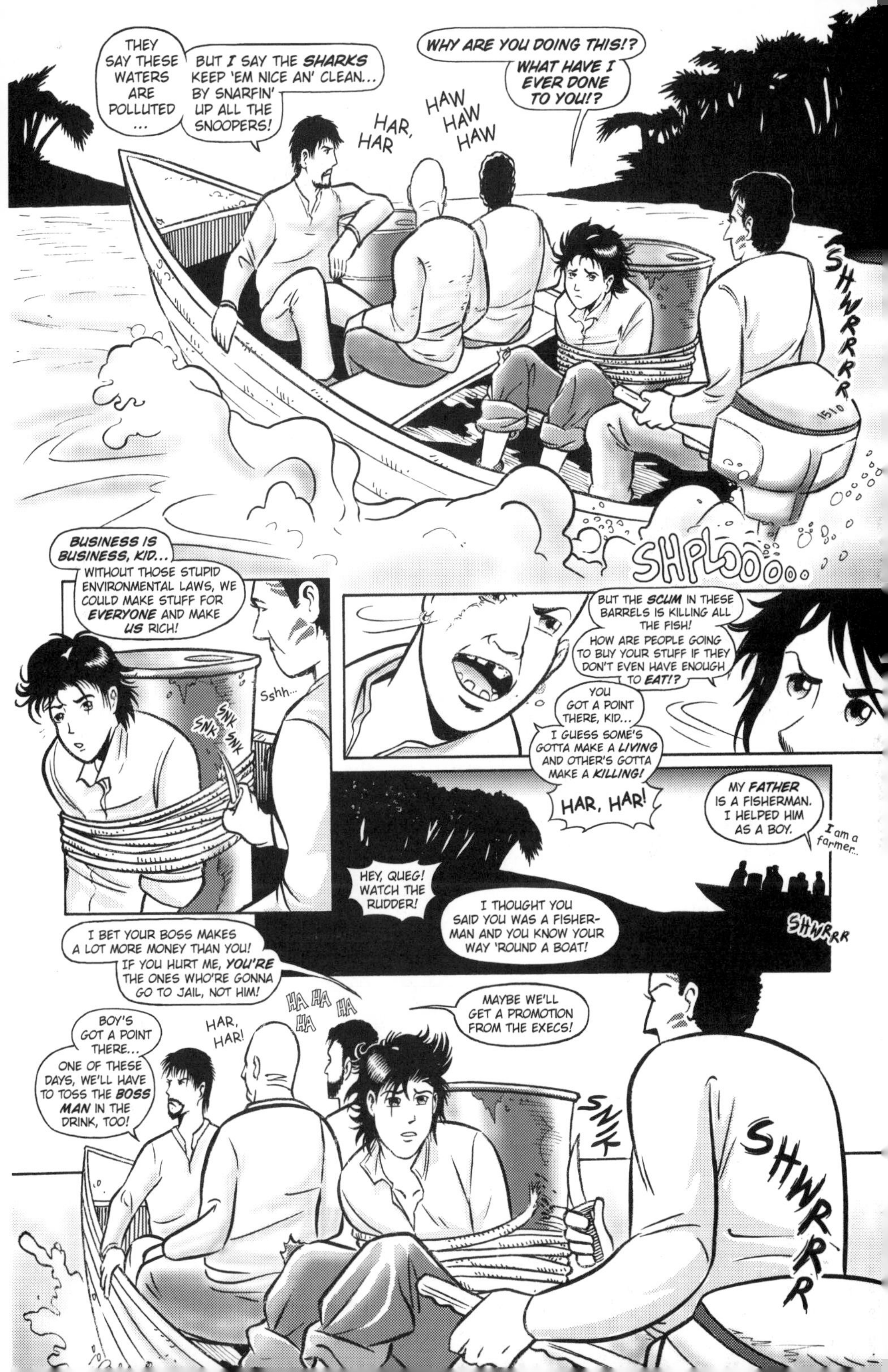

THEY SAY THESE WATERS ARE POLLUTED ...
BUT *I* SAY THE ***SHARKS*** KEEP 'EM NICE AN' CLEAN... BY SNARFIN' UP ALL THE SNOOPERS!
HAR, HAR
HAW HAW HAW
WHY ARE YOU DOING THIS!?
WHAT HAVE I EVER DONE TO YOU!?
SHWRRRR
SHPLOOOooo
BUSINESS IS BUSINESS, KID...
WITHOUT THOSE STUPID ENVIRONMENTAL LAWS, WE COULD MAKE STUFF FOR ***EVERYONE*** AND MAKE ***US*** RICH!
Sshh...
SNK SNK SNK
BUT THE ***SCUM*** IN THESE BARRELS IS KILLING ALL THE FISH!
HOW ARE PEOPLE GOING TO BUY YOUR STUFF IF THEY DON'T EVEN HAVE ENOUGH TO ***EAT!?***
YOU GOT A POINT THERE, KID...
I GUESS SOME'S GOTTA MAKE A ***LIVING*** AND OTHER'S GOTTA MAKE A ***KILLING!***
HAR, HAR!
MY ***FATHER*** IS A FISHERMAN. I HELPED HIM AS A BOY.
I am a farmer...
HEY, QUEG! WATCH THE RUDDER!
I THOUGHT YOU SAID YOU WAS A FISHER-MAN AND YOU KNOW YOUR WAY 'ROUND A BOAT!
SHWRRR
I BET YOUR BOSS MAKES A LOT MORE MONEY THAN YOU!
IF YOU HURT ME, ***YOU'RE*** THE ONES WHO'RE GONNA GO TO JAIL, NOT HIM!
BOY'S GOT A POINT THERE...
ONE OF THESE DAYS, WE'LL HAVE TO TOSS THE ***BOSS MAN*** IN THE DRINK, TOO!
HAR, HAR!
HA HA HA HA
MAYBE WE'LL GET A PROMOTION FROM THE EXECS!
SNIK
SHWRRRR

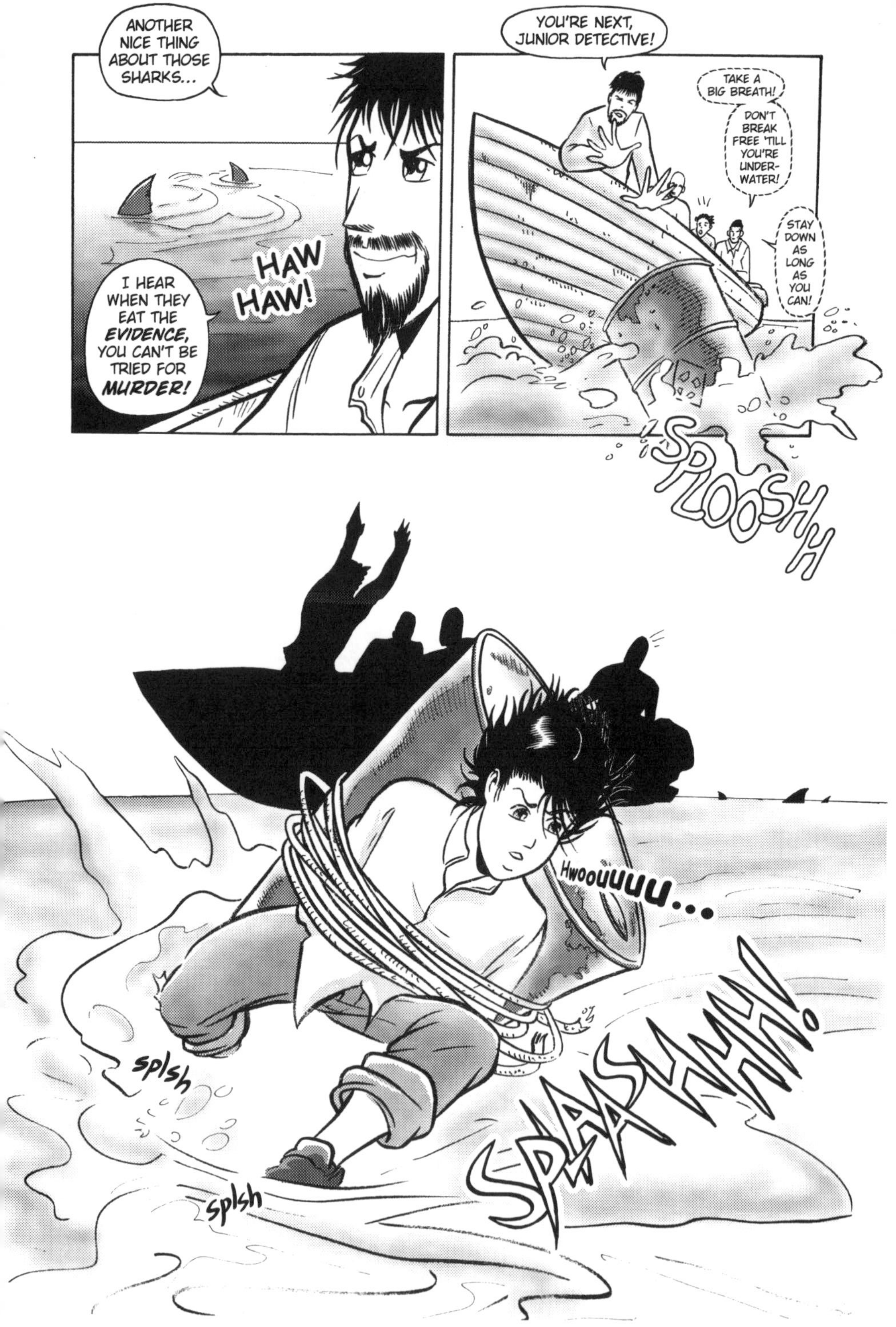
ANOTHER NICE THING ABOUT THOSE SHARKS...
HAW HAW!
I HEAR WHEN THEY EAT THE *EVIDENCE*, YOU CAN'T BE TRIED FOR *MURDER!*
YOU'RE NEXT, JUNIOR DETECTIVE!
TAKE A BIG BREATH!
DON'T BREAK FREE 'TILL YOU'RE UNDER-WATER!
STAY DOWN AS LONG AS YOU CAN!
SPLOOSHHH
Hwoouuuu...
SPLASHHH!
splsh
splsh

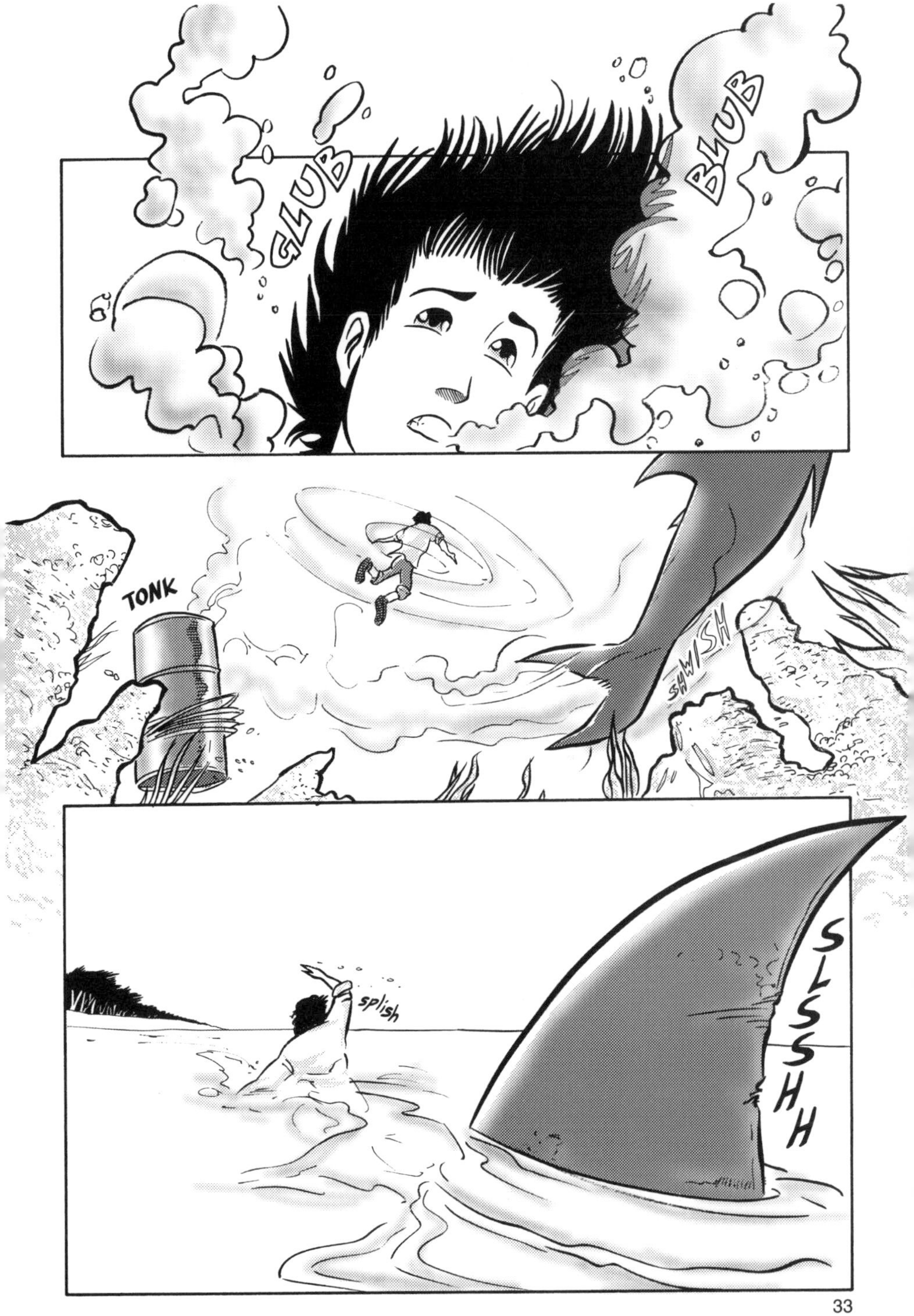
GLUB
BLUB
TONK
SHWISH
splish
SLSSHH

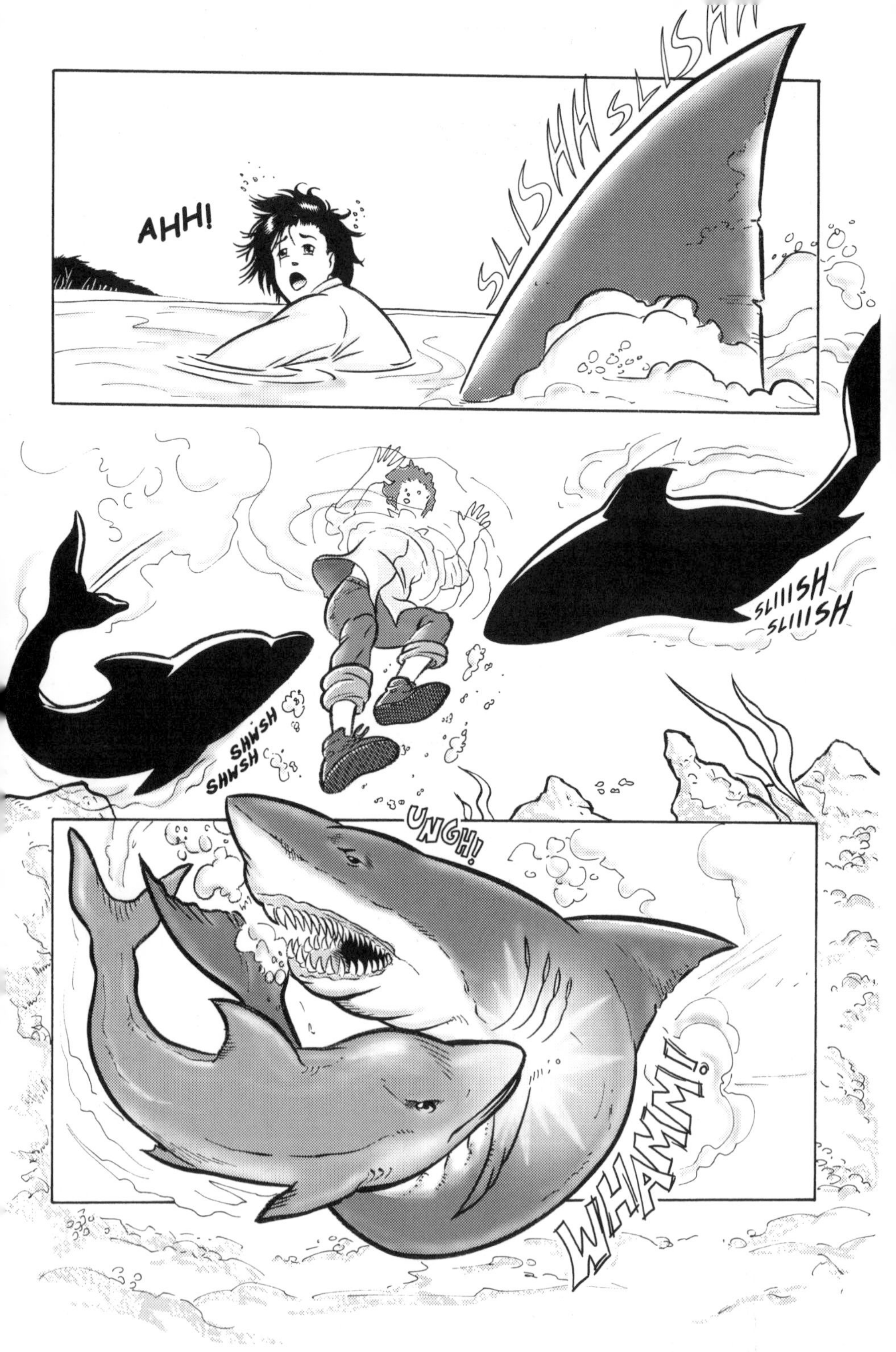
AHH!
SLISHH SLISH
SLIIISH SLIIISH
SHWSH SHWSH
UNGH!
WHAMM!

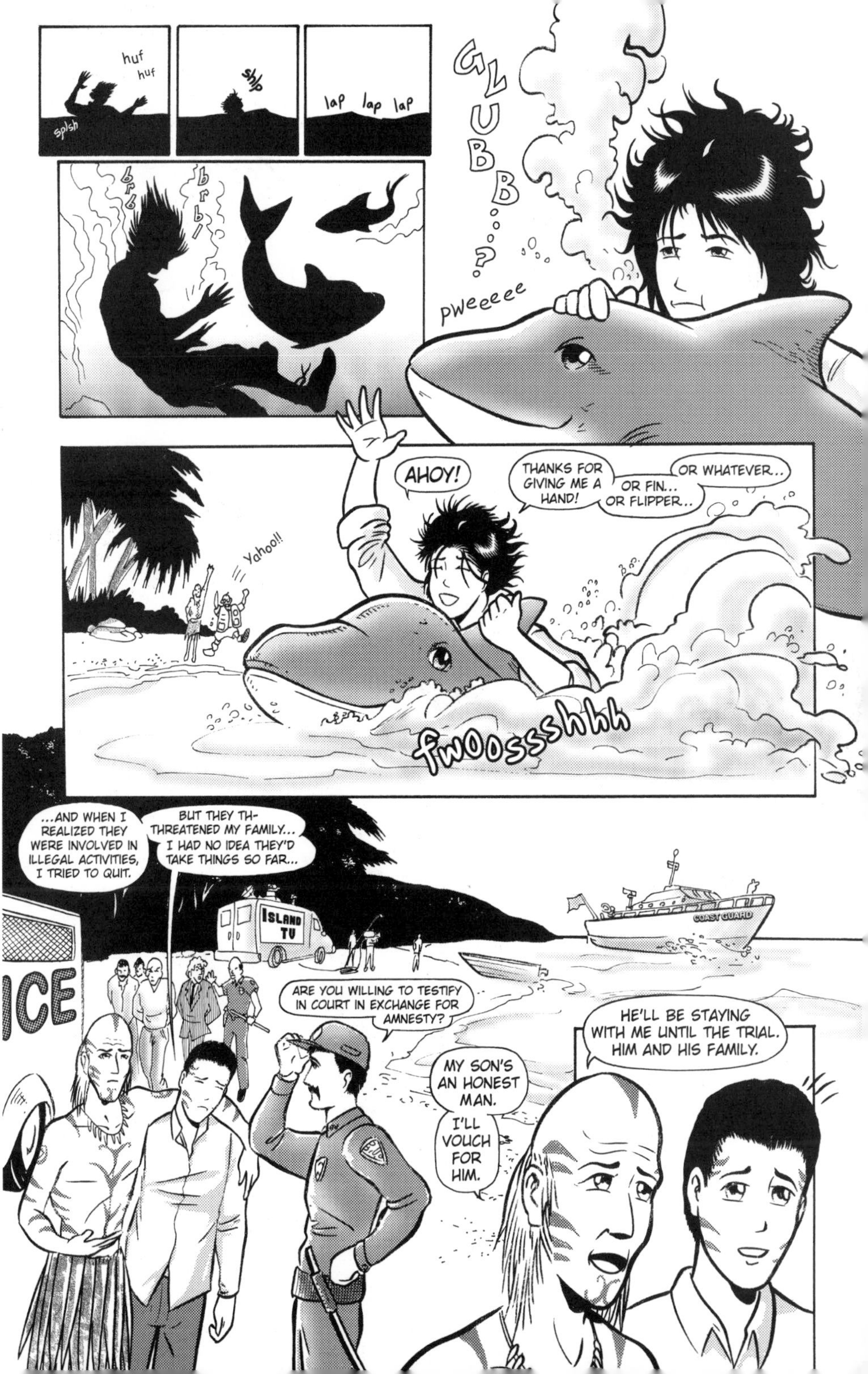
huf
huf
splsh
shlp
lap lap lap
brb
brbl
GLUBB...?
pweeeee
AHOY!
THANKS FOR GIVING ME A HAND!
OR FIN... OR FLIPPER...
OR WHATEVER...
Yahoo!!
fwoossshhh
...AND WHEN I REALIZED THEY WERE INVOLVED IN ILLEGAL ACTIVITIES, I TRIED TO QUIT.
BUT THEY TH-THREATENED MY FAMILY... I HAD NO IDEA THEY'D TAKE THINGS SO FAR...
ISLAND TV
COAST GUARD
ICE
ARE YOU WILLING TO TESTIFY IN COURT IN EXCHANGE FOR AMNESTY?
MY SON'S AN HONEST MAN.
I'LL VOUCH FOR HIM.
HE'LL BE STAYING WITH ME UNTIL THE TRIAL. HIM AND HIS FAMILY.

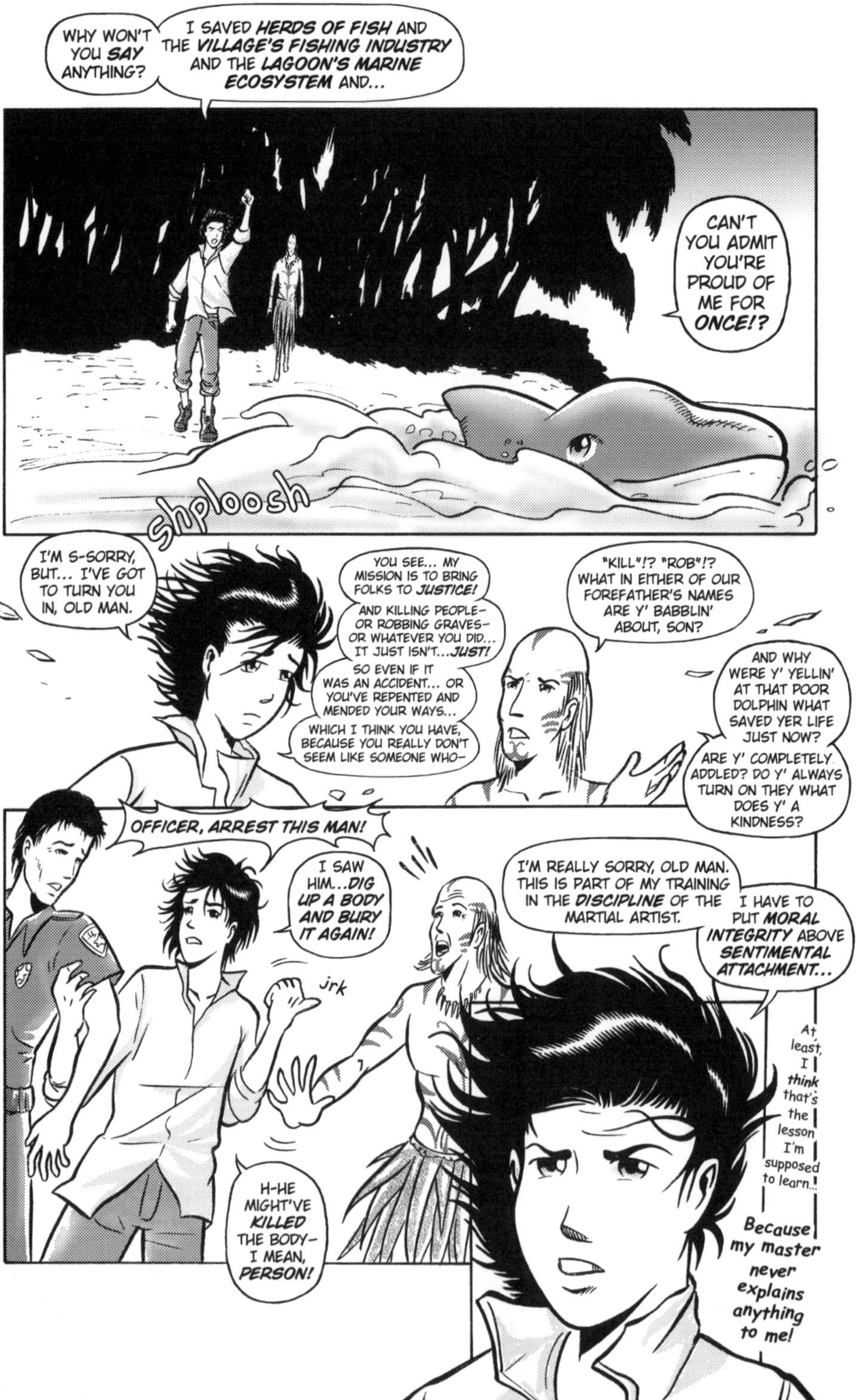
WHY WON'T YOU SAY ANYTHING?
I SAVED HERDS OF FISH AND THE VILLAGE'S FISHING INDUSTRY AND THE LAGOON'S MARINE ECOSYSTEM AND...
CAN'T YOU ADMIT YOU'RE PROUD OF ME FOR ONCE!?
shploosh
I'M S-SORRY, BUT... I'VE GOT TO TURN YOU IN, OLD MAN.
YOU SEE... MY MISSION IS TO BRING FOLKS TO JUSTICE!
AND KILLING PEOPLE- OR ROBBING GRAVES- OR WHATEVER YOU DID... IT JUST ISN'T...JUST!
SO EVEN IF IT WAS AN ACCIDENT... OR YOU'VE REPENTED AND MENDED YOUR WAYS...
WHICH I THINK YOU HAVE, BECAUSE YOU REALLY DON'T SEEM LIKE SOMEONE WHO-
"KILL"!? "ROB"!? WHAT IN EITHER OF OUR FOREFATHER'S NAMES ARE Y' BABBLIN' ABOUT, SON?
AND WHY WERE Y' YELLIN' AT THAT POOR DOLPHIN WHAT SAVED YER LIFE JUST NOW?
ARE Y' COMPLETELY ADDLED? DO Y' ALWAYS TURN ON THEY WHAT DOES Y' A KINDNESS?
OFFICER, ARREST THIS MAN!
I SAW HIM...DIG UP A BODY AND BURY IT AGAIN!
jrk
H-HE MIGHT'VE KILLED THE BODY- I MEAN, PERSON!
I'M REALLY SORRY, OLD MAN. THIS IS PART OF MY TRAINING IN THE DISCIPLINE OF THE MARTIAL ARTIST.
I HAVE TO PUT MORAL INTEGRITY ABOVE SENTIMENTAL ATTACHMENT...
At least, I think that's the lesson I'm supposed to learn...
Because my master never explains anything to me!

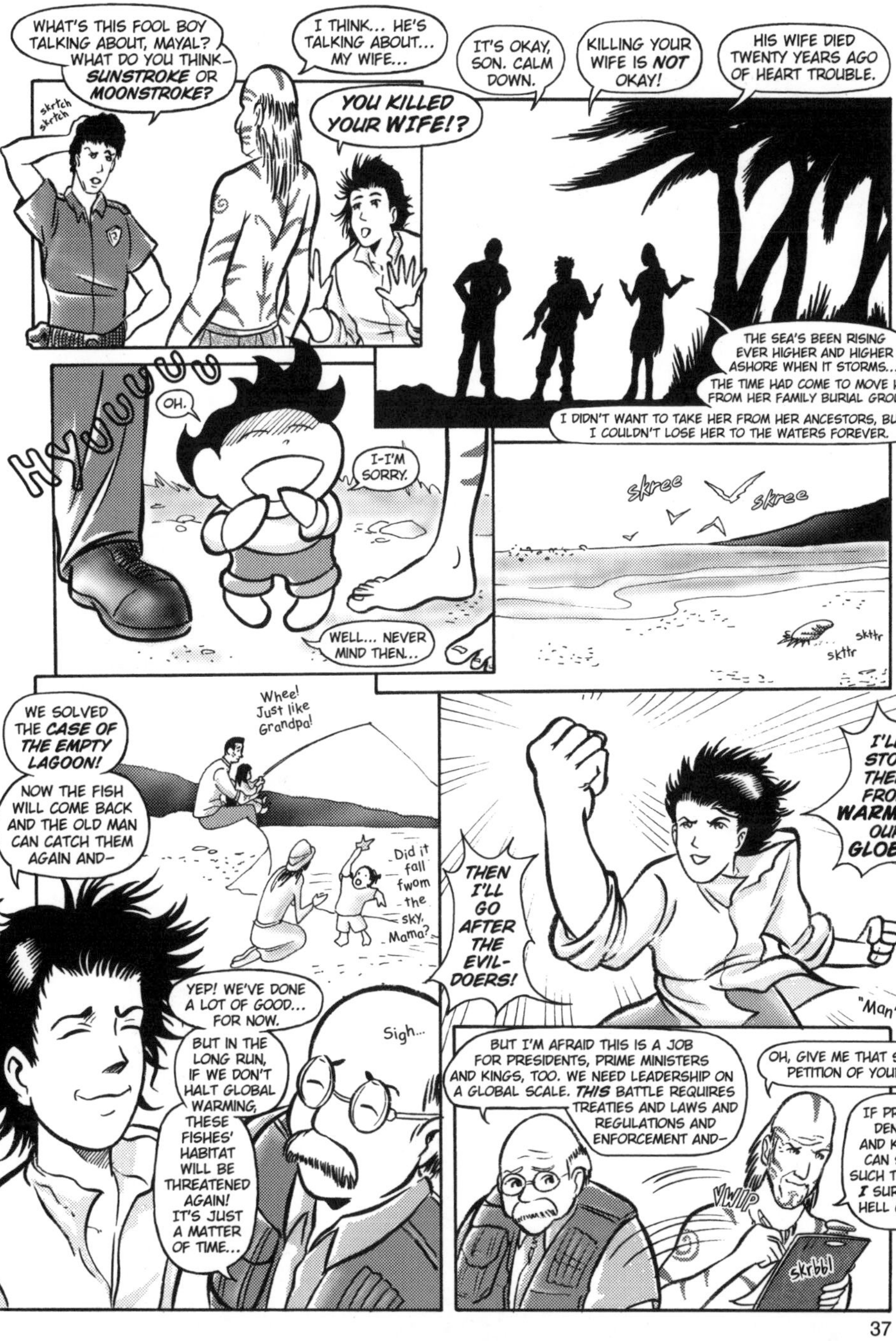

WHAT'S THIS FOOL BOY TALKING ABOUT, MAYAL? WHAT DO YOU THINK– SUNSTROKE OR MOONSTROKE?
skrtch skrtch
I THINK... HE'S TALKING ABOUT... MY WIFE...
YOU KILLED YOUR WIFE!?
IT'S OKAY, SON. CALM DOWN.
KILLING YOUR WIFE IS NOT OKAY!
HIS WIFE DIED TWENTY YEARS AGO OF HEART TROUBLE.
THE SEA'S BEEN RISING EVER HIGHER AND HIGHER ASHORE WHEN IT STORMS...
THE TIME HAD COME TO MOVE HER FROM HER FAMILY BURIAL GROUND.
I DIDN'T WANT TO TAKE HER FROM HER ANCESTORS, BUT... I COULDN'T LOSE HER TO THE WATERS FOREVER.
HYUUUUUU
OH.
I-I'M SORRY.
WELL... NEVER MIND THEN...
skree
skree
skttr
skttr
WE SOLVED THE CASE OF THE EMPTY LAGOON!
NOW THE FISH WILL COME BACK AND THE OLD MAN CAN CATCH THEM AGAIN AND–
Whee! Just like Grandpa!
Did it fall fwom the sky, Mama?
YEP! WE'VE DONE A LOT OF GOOD... FOR NOW.
BUT IN THE LONG RUN, IF WE DON'T HALT GLOBAL WARMING, THESE FISHES' HABITAT WILL BE THREATENED AGAIN! IT'S JUST A MATTER OF TIME...
Sigh...
I'LL STOP THEM FROM WARMING OUR GLOBE!
THEN I'LL GO AFTER THE EVIL-DOERS!
A MAN AFTER MY OWN HEART, REI!
"Man"!?
BUT I'M AFRAID THIS IS A JOB FOR PRESIDENTS, PRIME MINISTERS AND KINGS, TOO. WE NEED LEADERSHIP ON A GLOBAL SCALE. THIS BATTLE REQUIRES TREATIES AND LAWS AND REGULATIONS AND ENFORCEMENT AND–
OH, GIVE ME THAT STUPID PETITION OF YOURS!
IF PRESIDENTS AND KINGS CAN SIGN SUCH THINGS, I SURE AS HELL CAN!!
VWIP
skrbbl

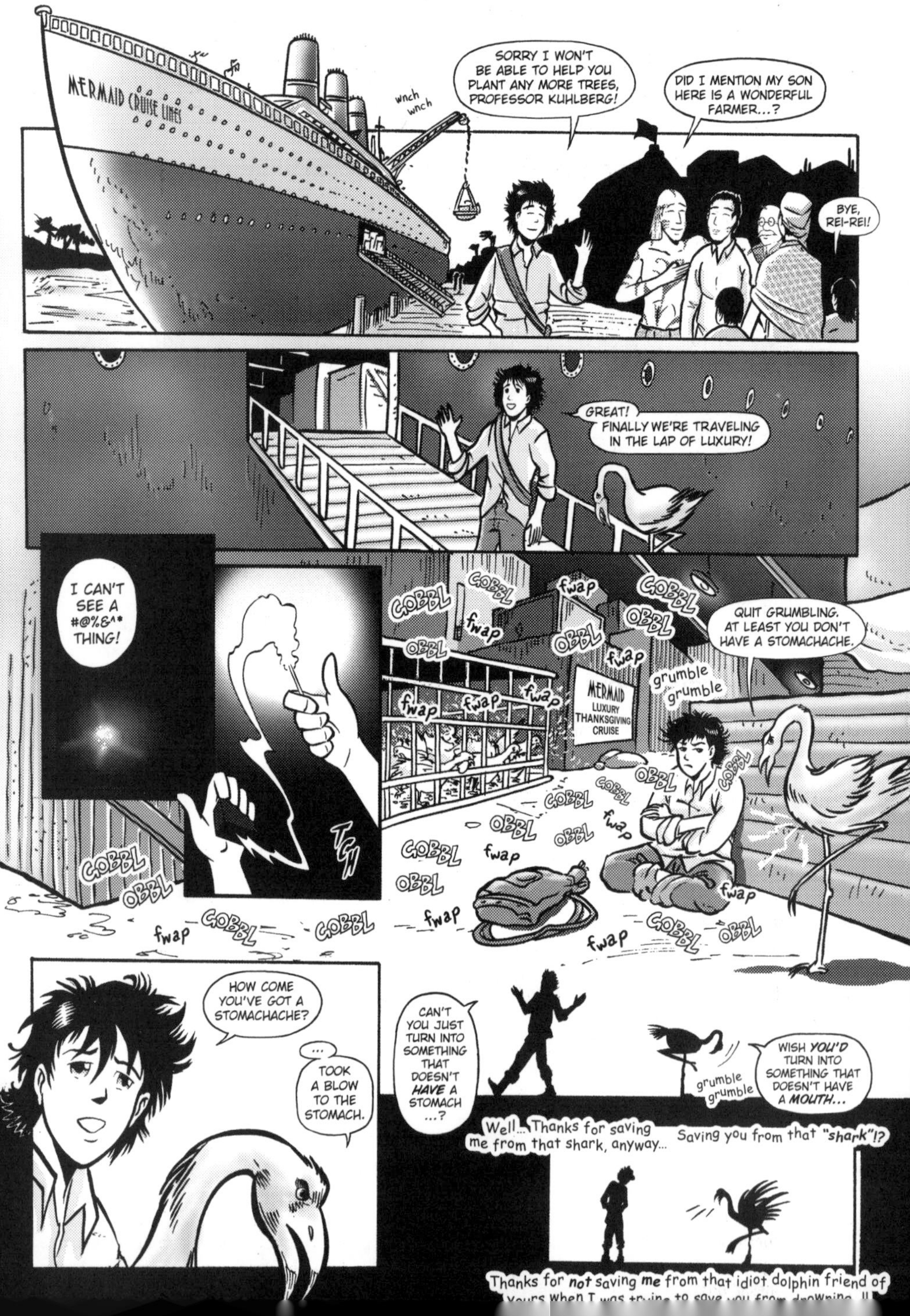

MERMAID CRUISE LINES
wnch wnch
SORRY I WON'T BE ABLE TO HELP YOU PLANT ANY MORE TREES, PROFESSOR KUHLBERG!
DID I MENTION MY SON HERE IS A WONDERFUL FARMER...?
BYE, REI-REI!
GREAT! FINALLY WE'RE TRAVELING IN THE LAP OF LUXURY!
I CAN'T SEE A #@%&^* THING!
TCH
GOBBL OBBL
GOBBL GOBBL fwap OBBL GOBBL OBBL fwap fwap fwap fwap
MERMAID LUXURY THANKSGIVING CRUISE
grumble grumble
QUIT GRUMBLING. AT LEAST YOU DON'T HAVE A STOMACHACHE.
GOBBL OBBL fwap GOBBL fwap GOBBL fwap OBBL fwap GOBBL OBBL fwap
HOW COME YOU'VE GOT A STOMACHACHE?
...
TOOK A BLOW TO THE STOMACH.
CAN'T YOU JUST TURN INTO SOMETHING THAT DOESN'T *HAVE* A STOMACH ...?
grumble grumble
WISH *YOU'D* TURN INTO SOMETHING THAT DOESN'T HAVE A **MOUTH...**
Well... Thanks for saving me from that shark, anyway...
Saving you from that "**shark**"!?
Thanks for **not** saving **me** from that idiot dolphin friend of yours when I was trying to save you from drowning..!!

OUR WORLD, 1 WORLD

GLOBAL WARMING AND GREEENHOUSE GASES

The majority of scientific experts agree that the earth's average temperature is rising as a result of human activities—driving vehicles, manufacturing, heating, electricity generation, and so on. A warmer earth can disrupt rainfall patterns, causing a rise in sea levels and leading to a host of other harmful effects on plants, animals, and humans. According to experts, average global temperatures are predicted to rise between 1.4 and 5.8 degrees Celsius over the next 100 years, a rate of warming higher than any that has occurred over the past 10,000 years!

What is the cause of this warming of the earth's climate? Over the past 50 years, the culprit has been greenhouse gas emissions. Since the industrial revolution, economic growth has depended on the consumption of fossil fuels—coal, oil, and natural gas that are burned by factories, electric power plants, cars, and households. The resulting carbon dioxide (CO_2) emissions are the largest source of the problem: greenhouse gases. These gasses trap the infrared radiation (heat) from the earth within its oxygen atmosphere and create global warming.

To learn more, check out:
• www.youthink.worldbank.org/issues/environment
• http://www.climateark.org/
• http://www.ipcc.ch/
• http://climatechange.unep.net/
• www.climate.wri.org

EFFECTS OF CLIMATE CHANGE

Changes in the earth's climate are harmful to the environment, people, and animals in a number of ways. Climate change can:

• Decrease water supplies and make water unsafe to drink in arid and semiarid regions
• Increase the risk of floods and droughts in many other regions
• Cause outbreaks of diseases like malaria, dengue, and cholera, especially in the tropics and subtropics
• Kill off the last of already vulnerable species forever (extinction)
• Harm the delicate ecosystems (balance of nature) in coral reefs, forests, grasslands, and high-mountain areas
• Trigger natural disasters, such as storms, hurricanes, and tornadoes
• Decrease farmers' ability to grow food and other plants they rely on to make a living in the tropics and sub-tropics
• Raise sea levels so that tens of millions of people living in low-lying areas are permanently flooded out of their homes and land
• Threaten the very existence of small low-lying island states

WHY THE POOR SUFFER THE MOST

Climate change poses extreme risks to developing countries because its effect on water, agriculture, forests, and fisheries has a direct impact on people's health and livelihoods. The Intergovernmental Panel on Climate Change (IPCC) has concluded that poor people living in developing countries are the most vulnerable to the effects of climate change. The IPCC estimates that a 3 degree Celsius increase in global temperatures could lead to a loss of gross domestic product (GDP) in developing countries of 2 to 9 percent per year. This loss of income and money would have a devastating impact on their population's health and welfare.

Why? Because it is developing countries that rely the most heavily on industries like agriculture, forestry, and fisheries, which are the most sensitive to changes in the climate. These countries also lack the technology, governmental institutions, and money to cope with changes in weather patterns. And the regions that are predicted to experience the greatest changes in climate—the tropics and subtropics—are where the majority of the world's poor live.

Sadly, most of the greenhouse gas emissions that cause these devastating climate changes come from wealthy industrialized countries. Emissions per person in a rich country are five times higher than that of a person in a poor country. With only 15 percent of the world's population, rich countries are responsible for more than 75 percent of global carbon dioxide emissions! The United States is the greatest contributor to global warming; although it is home to just 4 percent of the world's population, it produces almost a quarter of global CO_2 emissions. Unfortunately, developing countries are catching up—within 20 to 30 years, emissions from these countries—especially middle-income ones such as China, India, Brazil, Mexico, and South Africa—are expected to surpass those of rich countries.

INTERNATIONAL RESPONSES

At the 1992 Earth Summit in Rio de Janeiro, Brazil, many developed nations agreed to work toward stabilizing their greenhouse gas emissions at 1990 levels by the year 2000. In 1997, 165 countries gathered in Kyoto, Japan, for the United Nations Conference on Climate Change, where they developed The Kyoto Protocol, a legally binding document that calls on industrialized nations—which are responsible for the majority of emissions—to cut their greenhouse gas emissions by an average of 5.2 percent, with the goal of reaching levels below 1990 by 2012. As of February 26, 2005, when the Protocol went into force, 55 countries have ratified the Protocol.

To learn more, check out: http://unfccc.int/

WHAT CAN WE DO?

Our global community must reduce pollution from fossil fuels in ways that don't destroy economies and are fair to those countries that bear little responsibility for harmful CO_2 emissions. Our leaders, businesses, and communities should promote sustainable development—modernization that doesn't deplete or pollute resources—by supporting efforts to do the following:

• Switch to renewable energy sources such as wind, solar, and biofuels (fuels made from plant materials such as wood, farm waste, and ethanol) to provide our electricity
• Improve nature's ability to soak up carbon dioxide in the air by planting new forests and using new methods to encourage soil to absorb carbon
• Provide incentives for industries to be more fuel efficient by implementing national and international systems of buying and selling carbon emissions trading permits. (The box below shows how this works.)
• Encourage businesses to engage in projects in developing countries that use innovative climate-friendly technologies
• Conserve energy and improve energy efficiency by making power stations and factories run more efficiently, driving more fuel-efficient cars or using mass transportation, and better insulating buildings and homes